# Health and Society in Britain
## since 1939

# New Studies in Economic and Social History

*Edited for the Economic History Society by*
Michael Sanderson
*University of East Anglia, Norwich*

This series, specially commissioned by the Economic History Society, provides a guide to the current interpretations of the key themes of economic and social history in which advances have recently been made or in which there has been significant debate.

In recent times economic and social history has been one of the most flourishing areas of historical study. This has mirrored the increasing relevance of the economic and social sciences both in a student's choice of career and in forming a society at large more aware of the importance of these issues in their everyday lives. Moreover specialist interests in business, agricultural and welfare history, for example, have themselves burgeoned and there has been an increased interest in the economic development of the wider world. Stimulating as these scholarly developments have been for the specialist, the rapid advance of the subject and the quantity of new publications make it difficult for the reader to gain an overview of particular topics, let alone the whole field.

*New Studies in Economic and Social History* is intended for students and their teachers. It is designed to introduce them to fresh topics and to enable them to keep abreast of recent writing and debates. All the books in the series are written by a recognised authority in the subject, and the arguments and issues are set out in a critical but unpartisan fashion. The aim of the series is to survey the current state of scholarship, rather than to provide a set of pre-packaged conclusions.

The series has been edited since its inception in 1968 by Professors M. W. Flinn, T. C. Smout and L. A. Clarkson, and is currently edited by Dr Michael Sanderson. From 1968 it was published by Macmillan as *Studies in Economic History*, and after 1974 as *Studies in Economic and Social History*. From 1995 *New Studies in Economic and Social History* is being published on behalf of the Economic History Society by Cambridge University Press. This new series includes some of the titles previously published by Macmillan as well as new titles, and reflects the ongoing development throughout the world of this rich seam of history.

*For a full list of titles in print, please see the end of the book.*

# Health and Society in Britain since 1939

*Prepared for the Economic History Society by*

## Virginia Berridge
*London School of Hygiene and Tropical Medicine*

CAMBRIDGE
UNIVERSITY PRESS

PUBLISHED BY THE PRESS SYNDICATE OF THE UNIVERSITY OF
CAMBRIDGE
The Pitt Building, Trumpington Street, Cambridge CB2 1RP, United
Kingdom

CAMBRIDGE UNIVERSITY PRESS
The Edinburgh Building, Cambridge CB2 2RU, United
Kingdom   http://www.cup.cam.ac.uk
40 West 20th Street, New York, NY 10011-4211,
USA   http://www.cup.org
10 Stamford Road, Oakleigh, Melbourne 3166, Australia

© The Economic History Society 1999   ᔑ ⋀ ᥴ

First published 1999   362 . 1  BER

Printed in the United Kingdom at the University Press, Cambridge

Typeset in Plantin 10/12.5 pt [VN]

*A catalogue record for this book is available from the British Library*

*Library of Congress cataloguing in publication data*

Berridge, Virginia.
   Health and society in Britain since 1939 / prepared for the Economic
History Society by Virginia Berridge.
      p.      cm. – (New studies in economic and social history)
   Includes bibliographical references and index.
   ISBN 0 521 57230 4 (hb)
   ISBN 0 521 57641 5 (pb)
   1. Health – Social aspects – Great Britain – History 20th century.
2. Medical care – Social aspects – Great Britain – History 20th century.
3. Medical policy – Social aspects – Great Britain – History 20th century.
4. Social medicine – Great Britain – History 20th century. 5. Public
health – Social aspects – Great Britain – History 20th century. 6.
Medicine – Social aspects – Great Britain – History 20th century. I.
Title. II. Series.
   R486.B47 1999
   362.1'042'09410904–ddc21      98–43280 CIP

ISBN 0 521 57230 4 hardback
ISBN 0 521 57641 5 paperback

# Contents

# Acknowledgements

Although this is a short text, many people have helped in its gestation. Jane Lewis, Jenny Stanton, Pat Thane and Charles Webster read the manuscript and offered good advice. Discussions with colleagues at the London School of Hygiene and Tropical Medicine informed the more recent chapters. Martin McKee and Charles Normand gave advice on, respectively, European health data and health service statistics. Simon Szreter clarified a demographic issue. My thanks are also due to Michael Thompson for involving me in the *Cambridge Social History of Britain*, where I first surveyed the historiography of the coming of the NHS; and to Charles Webster for enrolling me as a member of the course team for the Open University text, *Caring for Health. History and Diversity*. These previous surveys were the springboard for the present text, and I have adapted the latter book's post-war organisation for use here. Thanks to many of the authors cited for sending reprints and for letting me look at pre-publication copies of books and articles, and especially to Geoffrey Rivett and Charles Webster for the chance to read MS copies of their histories of the NHS. As always, libraries – those of LSHTM, the London School of Economics, and the Wellcome Institute – have been a valuable resource. An anonymous referee and the overall Editor of the series, Dr Michael Sanderson, offered excellent editorial suggestions. My final thanks are to Ingrid James for secretarial support.

Tables 1 and 2 are taken from J. Charlton and M. Murphy (eds.), *The Health of Adult Britain 1841–1994* (London: Stationery Office, 1997), with the permission of the Office for National Statistics. Table 3 is taken from the WHO Health for All database and compiled by Martin McKee. Tables 4 and 5 are taken from the Office of Health Economics (OHE), *Compendium of Health Statistics* (London: OHE, 8th edn, 1992) with permission.

# Abbreviations

| | |
|---|---|
| AHA | Area Health Authority |
| ASTMS | Association of Scientific, Technical and Managerial Staff (now MSF) |
| BMA | British Medical Association |
| CCHE | Central Council for Health Education |
| CHC | Community Health Council |
| COHSE | Confederation of Health Service Employees |
| CMO | Chief Medical Officer |
| COMA | Committee on the Medical Aspects of Food Policy |
| CSD | Committee on the Safety of Drugs |
| DHA | District Health Authority |
| DHSS | Department of Health and Social Security |
| EAGA | Expert Advisory Group on AIDS |
| FHSA | Family Health Services Authority |
| GDP | gross domestic product |
| GP | general practitioner |
| HA | Health Authority |
| HEA | Health Education Authority |
| HEC | Health Education Council |
| HFA | Health for All |
| HRT | hormone replacement therapy |
| LCC | London County Council |
| LSE | London School of Economics |
| LSHTM | London School of Hygiene and Tropical Medicine |
| MoH | Medical Officer of Health |
| MPU | Medical Practitioners' Union |
| MRC | Medical Research Council |
| NACNE | National Advisory Committee on Nutrition Education |
| NHS | National Health Service |

| | |
|---|---|
| NHSME | National Health Service Management Executive |
| NUPE | National Union of Public Employees |
| PEP | Political and Economic Planning |
| PESC | Public Expenditure Survey Committee |
| QALY | quality-adjusted life year |
| RAWP | Resource Allocation Working Party |
| RCN | Royal College of Nursing |
| RCP | Royal College of Physicians |
| RCT | randomised controlled trial |
| SIDS | Sudden Infant Death Syndrome |
| TB | tuberculosis |
| TFR | total fertility rate |
| VD | venereal disease |
| WHO | World Health Organisation |
| *YLITH* | *Your Life in Their Hands* |

# 1
# Introduction: historiographical contexts. Writing about the war and post-war period

This book examines responses to health and sickness at a number of different levels – lay, medical and political – in Britain in the period from the outbreak of the Second World War and through the post-war period into the 1990s. Its focus is broader than the issue of the development of health services, which has so far attracted the lion's share of historians' attention. The latter interest has perhaps reflected the increasing twentieth-century preoccupation with the delivery of such services (Lewis, 1992 a). But the focus of this book enables questions to be asked about issues of continuity and of change. It also enables an examination of what is currently called the 'mixed economy' of health care, the shifting configuration between different 'providers' of health care, and their relationships with both the recipients of care and the state. One way of characterising the period overall is of the post-war rise, and recent decline, of the National Health Service (NHS). This is a common media representation of this period of health history at the time of writing. But there are other health issues at a wider level. The book will examine the changing balances of power within the medical profession, but also between the profession, the state and its agents of non-medical control. Its concern is also with a traditional area of health care, that provided by lay people, and especially by women. Their role has undergone considerable development in the light of recent policy changes. The concept of prevention, so important in the interwar discussions of health care reform, has been redefined in the post-war period to mean the individual's responsibility for health. Behind these issues also lie questions of costs which have become increasingly prominent, although also of importance since the earliest days of the service. Containing costs while maintaining the economic value of a healthy population has been a continuing theme. Increasingly the focus of debate has shifted from the inputs to the outputs of medical care. The relationship of the latter to health status, and its measurement, has moved centre stage.

The book combines chronological and thematic approaches. Chapter 2, starting where the previous survey volume by Cherry left off, considers the wartime changes in health services and the establishment of the NHS in 1946–8. What impact did the war have on the development of services? How far did the subsequent NHS represent the outgrowth of consensus between the parties? The post-war period was initially a time of expansion and full employment, a period of optimistic faith in the power of medical science and of curative medicine. This expansionism was abruptly ended by the oil crisis of 1973 which brought a general period of retrenchment in the welfare state, with a reorientation and reconsideration of the role of health services both in Britain and internationally. The major subsections of the text take 1974 as their dividing year, both because of this decisive change and because of the change in government in Britain.

Chapter 3 covers the years of the post-war Labour governments, their Conservative successors (1951–64), the Labour governments (1964–70) and the Conservative government led by Edward Heath (1970–74). The first section (pp. 23–34) considers the way in which the organisation of health services has developed over this period. How did the optimism of the 1950s and 60s and the faith in high technology give place to an emphasis on cost cutting and 'organisational fixes'? The continuing role of lay care is the subject of the second section (pp. 34–41). What did the emergent concept of 'community care' mean in practice and how did care in the community become care by the community? What patterns of lay involvement in health care continued – and expanded? What implications did lay care have for the involvement of women, who had historically provided care within the family? The third section (pp. 41–48) examines the development of the medical profession in the post-war period and its relationship with other health care occupations such as nursing. What were the tensions within the profession between, for example, GPs and public health doctors, or GPs and consultants? How were balances of power shifting in this period? Public health, historically both a medical occupation and an area of health intervention, is the subject of the fourth section (pp. 48–54). How was the nature of public health being redefined in the post-war period? What impact did the loss of the formal public health empire in 1948 and further changes in 1974 have on what had traditionally been seen as public health activity?

Chapter 4 takes the analysis forward in those same areas after 1974 and into the 1990s, covering the period of the Labour government of 1974–9, followed by the Conservatives (1979–97). Reorganisation and the control of costs were again dominant themes within health services. Lay care appeared to undergo a further revival as part of government redefinitions of community care. The balance of power between the health professions was again in a state of flux. How far had clinical autonomy and the doctor/patient relationship been eroded by interventions from the state and other non-medical health occupations? What role did management really play? And how far was public health really redefining its role in the 1980s and 90s? Did the apparent revival of infectious disease presage new initiatives in public health, or were older themes and tendencies simply relaunched? The issue of inequalities had failed to be addressed by Conservative governments of the 80s and 90s, but was re-emergent at the time of writing. How far did the issue of the public's health and its variation conflict with the assumed agendas adopted by 'professional' public health?

These are areas of current debate, and not solely among historians of health. The post-war period is one which has very obviously shaped the present, and, as the century draws to a close, it is natural to look back and to reflect. Many commentators have done this. But the period from the 1950s to the 1990s remains comparatively virgin territory for health historians. This is perhaps surprising. The end of the war is over half a century away and the public records are open officially up to the mid 1960s. Surveys of post-war politics have proliferated and the study of 'contemporary history' is an expanding field. Yet often such surveys treat health in a cursory way. The broader approach to health policy has fallen uneasily between the 'social policy' and the 'high politics' schools of writing and research. Major research studies by historians have been rare, with work by Webster and Lewis predominant (Webster, 1988a and b; Lewis, 1986, 1992a). The publication of volume two of the former's official history of the NHS as this book was in draft underlined the richness of material potentially available (Webster, 1996). Demographic research is also expanding into the post-war period (Winter, 1983; Loudon 1991). Synthetic work by historians dealing either specifically with health (Jones, 1994) or more generally with the history of the welfare state (Lowe, 1993; Gladstone, 1995) is beginning to appear. The neglected clinical and scientific aspects of medical care are beginning to be covered (Lawrence, 1994; Rivett, 1998). Much of this work has been invaluable for the synthesis presented here and is given in-depth consideration later in the text.

Many historians are uneasy with anything beyond the 1960s, where the usual boundaries between primary and secondary source material largely break down. 'Journalist histories' have provided excellent surveys, although tending to focus on the 'high politics' of health rather than the less gossipy foothills (Timmins, 1995). Much valuable literature can be found in the work of policy scientists and of medical sociologists and social administration specialists (Allsop, 1995a and b; Baggott, 1994; Glennerster, 1995; Ham, 1992; Hills, 1991; Klein, 1995; Stacey, 1988). Some recent studies usefully integrate a multidisciplinary approach, including that of historians (Oakley and Williams, 1994). It could be argued that historians are only just beginning to realise the possibilities of the last thirty or so years and of the use of established methods such as oral history (Berridge, 1996).

The advantages of this varied literature are many, not least because they enable historical consideration of both macro and micro theories of policy making, together with an awareness of the nature of power in pluralist societies. Lowe (1993, pp. 9–61) provides an excellent introductory guide to types of theoretical approaches deriving from economics, political science and social administration, which can help structure and inform historical work on the welfare state and health in particular. Issues such as the nature and role of bureaucracy, the implementation as well as the making of policy, the role of 'policy communities' or 'issue networks' in the making of policy are important considerations for historical work. Lowe discusses the predominant theory of pluralism, which assumes that power is diffused in society, with, in the case of health care, the state and government mediating between the consumers of health care (the public) and its producers (the medical profession). Clearly such a theory is open to objection; and other writers, especially those who focus on the NHS, have referred to 'corporatism' in policy making–power sharing between the state and powerful interest groups such as the medical profession (Klein, 1995), or to the role of privatisation and the interests of capital. Work deriving from a welfare state perspective has found the NHS a 'social democratic' entity in an otherwise liberal welfare state (Esping-Anderson, 1990). Feminist theory has added a further dimension, stressing the reinforcement of the dominance of men over women through the agencies of the welfare state, health services among them. This critique gained particular strength in the 1970s and will be discussed below. Most interpreters of health policy in the post-war period have, with reservations, seen the pluralistic standpoint as the best available initial premise for analysis.

All history is political, in particular that relating to health. But the immediacy of the war and especially the post-war period means that the political and policy context of debate has been more central. It has meant that formal health services and how they are to be, and have been, provided, have been centre stage. What are the major debates? Historians and policy scientists have joined battle over the concept of consensus and its applicability to the emergence of the NHS (Webster, 1990; Klein, 1995). The 'progressive history' of welfarism, implying a linear development of the welfare state out of earlier patchwork voluntary and state provision, has given place to a greater historical understanding of the shifting boundaries between different forms of health care provision, and in particular between voluntary and statutory care. Feminist historians and sociologists have ensured that the role of women as carers, as the recipients of medical intervention and as activists in health pressure groups, has been recognised. The changing historical role of old people, a matter of some concern for social policy, has also received historical attention. Historians have analysed how the 'problem' of an ageing population has been constructed (Jefferys, 1989; Thane, 1990, 1993). Debate has also focused on the nature of the 1990s health care reforms. Did the willingness of the government to attack the autonomy of the medical profession and to consider a reduction in the role of the state mark a radical change in health policy making and a new framework for services?

Many areas more remote from formal health services remain to be researched, although this text has attempted to encompass those areas through other forms of available research. There has been little by historians, although more by sociologists and anthropologists (Blaxter, 1990; Cornwell, 1984; Helman, 1990) on the more informal aspects of health and of popular health cultures. The developing historical interest in consumption and its theories and the relationship to health is as yet only weakly represented in the post-war work (Obelkevitch and Catterall, 1994). More work is currently in train and the next few years should see an expansion of health-related research-based studies of the post-war period (Webster, 1998). Historians who approach the present day in their work must deal with a dearth of historical writing, but a superabundance of 'primary source material' in terms of the outputs of health researchers. Such work has been drawn upon here, but selectively; it would require full text book coverage to do it justice.

## Demographic contexts: mortality, morbidity and population changes

What were the trends in mortality and morbidity during this period? Time series of deaths and rates for different ages and sex groups are readily obtainable (McPherson and Coleman, 1988; Charlton and Murphy, 1997). But it is more difficult to analyse death rates by cause of death over time because definitions of diseases have changed and at different times, different diseases have been classified in different ways. The late twentieth century has brought the UK and most other Western populations close to the end of a mortality transition from high to low death rates which began in the eighteenth century. There has been a radical switch in the major causes of death and the age at which most deaths occur. It has been argued that there is no evidence for any increase in natural life span and that the peak age of mortality is still within a few years of what it was in 1841, but this issue is contentious. What has happened is the reduction of premature deaths and the development of a 'rectangular curve' of mortality where more and more deaths are concentrated at old age (McPherson and Coleman, 1988, p. 399). Table 1 shows trends in crude death rates from 1941 to 1994 and the rising expectation of life at birth, a better measure of the level and trend in mortality risk. Smith (1994) posits the notion of a demographic regime of low birth rates, low mortality and population ageing. Trends in population growth can be divided in two, with the 1970s again as the dividing decade. Population grew rapidly in the decades after the Second World War, but since the 1970s, the rate has slowed markedly (Allsop, 1995b).

Tranter, examining the twentieth century overall, sees the greatest advances in life expectancy achieved in infancy (0–1) and childhood (1–4) and, to a lesser extent, among adolescents and young adults (15–24) and adults (25–44). For these groups, the bulk of the improvement was achieved by mid-century. In older age groups, up to those aged 65–74 mortality fell from the beginning of the twentieth century, but most of the decline did not occur until the second half of the century. Death rates among those over 80 did not begin to decline until the 1940s (Tranter, 1996, p. 67). In the post-war period, so far as mortality was concerned, two age groups, as Smith notes, benefited disproportionately. Infants experienced a fall of nearly 75% in their mortality rates from 1940 to 1980. The most rapid change occurred in the 1940s. The potential for further rapid improvement now seems to be severely limited. Of deaths after the first week of life, almost 40% are now categorised as 'cot death' or Sudden Infant Death Syndrome (SIDS). The causes here have been highly contentious and have been attributed to a range of factors from 'maternal ignorance' to inequalities in health. Evidence presented in the 1990s indicated that a high proportion of such deaths had been brought about by incorrect medical advice about sleeping postures and keeping infants over-warm. Britain's place in the international league table of infant mortality has deteriorated recently, as table 3 demonstrates.

The population was changing its age structure. The proportion of those under 16 declined, and those in the pensionable age groups increased. Old people also experienced improvements in their survival chances. Some of the historical debates concerned with this continuing trend are discussed below (chapter 3, second section, (pp. 34–7). Among the elderly, the post-war period has also witnessed a continuation and intensification of the advantage experienced by elderly females by comparison with those of elderly males, although recently this gender gap has tended to narrow. Webster (1996, p. 753) notes that, by 1979, of the total population of the

UK, 12% of men and 17.5% of women were over 65; 5.5% of the population were over 75 and 1% over 85. Such changes were not accompanied by a lessening of inequalities in health. Allsop (1995b) notes the continuing diversity of health experience of the population. Although all classes participated in the improvements in life expectancy, higher classes profited most of all. These trends have been debated, but social and geographical differentials in mortality can be seen to be increasing (Smith, 1994). What was subsequently termed 'variations in health' re-emerged as an area of concern in the 1990s.

Overall there has been a shift in the composition of causes of death, away from a pattern where infectious disease predominated towards deaths from chronic conditions such as cancer and the circulatory diseases. To some extent their predominance, as McPherson and Coleman (1988) argue, may relate to the decline of infectious disease. But circulatory disease and cancer mortality also have dynamics of their own. Until the 1960s, the death rates from these conditions were increasing, and they were regarded as inevitable consequences of the process of ageing. But a decline in death rates in the US as well as in the UK and elsewhere to a lesser extent led to the view that they were in part avoidable consequences of personal lifestyle and behaviour. These trends in mortality have been linked with the growth of the concept of personal prevention, which is discussed below.

Movements in fertility rates have been more influential than mortality shifts in determining population trends (Smith, 1994). The interpretation of fertility trends requires consideration of a number of interlinked areas such as social and sexual attitudes, the family and the status of women. Fertility rates rose between 1940 and 1964, and have thereafter fallen. Current total fertility rates (TFR) of around 1.8 are below replacement. (TFR has to be two or more for a couple to replace themselves.) Winter argues that these wartime and post-war fertility movements were part of 'the revival of family life' in the wake of the disruption of the Second World War. The 'baby boom' of the late 1950s and early 1960s was common to all countries in the developing world, but nowhere as pronounced as in Britain. In the second half of the 1960s, the baby boom was replaced by a 'baby bust' (Tranter, 1996). The earlier decline of fertility was resumed and only reversed in the late 1970s.

By 1990, birth rates were only slightly higher than a decade earlier. What lay behind these patterns of fertility? Tranter (p. 115) points out that periods of rising or stable post-war fertility were also periods of advance in the extent and efficacy of birth control. The availability of contraception cannot be given primary responsibility, although birth control, and especially the pill, did make a contribution to the reduction in family size. He traces a change in the way fertility responds to economic growth. Until the mid-1960s, fertility rates increased in times of economic growth. But since the mid-1960s, the relationship has changed to a negative one. Whenever real incomes have risen and unemployment fallen, fertility rates have decreased, not increased. He argues that the best explanation of this pattern lies in the proportion of married women employed outside the home and in the rates of men's to women's wages. Lewis (1992b) also notes that these were trends which specially affected women; the increasing percentage of married women in paid employment; the dramatic increase in the divorce rate in the 1970s and 80s (after the post-war 'marriage boom'); and a rise in illegitimacy from the 1960s. There was an increase in one-parent families, 90% of which were headed by women. Such households were associated particularly with marital breakdown. Anderson (summarised in Thane, 1989) has argued that this is not a 'new' social phenomenon. Marital breakdown rates in the nineteenth century were not very different, with the main difference being that it was death rather than divorce which caused lone parenthood. But in the post-war years, the link between marriage and childbirth began to be broken (Royle, 1994). The proportion of registered illegitimate births rose from 4.9% in the early 1950s to 31.7% by 1991. In 1988, the traditional family pattern of a married couple and children applied to only 26% of British households. But fears of the 'decline of the traditional family' were perhaps misplaced. In the 1950s only one third of registered illegitimate births had both parents' names on the birth certificate. By 1991, three-quarters listed both parents. Around half that number were registrations by parents living at the same address. Reliance on marriage had changed rather than 'the family' itself as a social unit. People still lived together and had children – but fewer of them saw marriage as essential to the creation of a family unit. Demographers have debated how and why these changes occurred (Smith, 1994).

# 2
# Health and the Second World War

Before looking at how these fundamental changes affected the post-war period, we first need to examine how health services – and also the health experience of the population – were affected by the Second World War. By the outbreak of war in 1939, there was no lack of knowledge of the chaotic and uncoordinated nature of health services in terms of distribution, access, financing and much else (Cherry, 1996). The patchwork of services included voluntary hospitals on the point of bankruptcy, insurance coverage which largely excluded dependants, and low morale among both GPs and consultants, together with the local authority-based public health service, which had taken on some Poor Law medical functions in the 1930s. In 1937, a Political and Economic Planning (PEP) report on *The British Health Services* underlined how 'a bewildering variety of agencies, official and unofficial, have been created during the past two or three generations to work for health mainly by attacking specific diseases and disabilities as they occur' (quoted in Pater, 1981 p. 19). Disease-specific services were extended when the 1939 Cancer Act laid the foundations for diagnosis organised by local authorities with coordination at regional level (there were already public TB and VD services). This emphasis on regional organisation foreshadowed the later NHS. The existing pattern of private and voluntary services, of public and local authority provision, could not effectively satisfy the need for health care, even if, as recent research has shown, the pre-war service was more responsive than once thought (Powell, 1997). Although some local authority services for example in London were comparable to later provision under the National Health Service, the areas of greatest need, as Webster has noted, were least able to sustain effective health and social services (Webster, 1988a, p. 8).

Already before the war, there was a growing demand for change. The Socialist Medical Association was pressing for a free National Health Service; in 1930 and again in 1938, the British Medical Association issued *A General Medical Service for the Nation* which suggested a system of health insurance for nearly all adults and their dependants. Pre-1939 suggestions, the impact of war and the subsequent Labour government upon the character of the National Health Service are important historical questions. Less attention has been paid to the wider impact of the war on civilian health and the relationship between health and the war effort. Both areas, health services and civilian health, are the focus of this chapter.

*The NHS: conflict or consensus?*

The debate about the coming of the National Health Service is part of the wider analysis of the impact of the war on the development of the post-war welfare state. It has also been inextricably bound up with the political science concept of consensus. The existence of a consensus round the need for a national health service, formerly a generally accepted orthodoxy, has recently been questioned. The established view of the NHS was that wartime experience led to new attitudes towards welfare policy (Titmuss, 1950). War forced government to take on new responsibilities and the evidence of poverty which the war brought to light, especially among evacuees, stimulated the mood for social reform. The spirit of 'never again' which animated post-war welfare was forged at both public and political levels during the Second World War. Reasoning that the war was the decisive element in stimulating social change, is echoed in some of the earlier histories of the health service. This belief in wartime solidarity still held true at a public and political level in 1995 when celebrations of the fiftieth anniversary of the end of the war took place. The NHS has been seen as the product of consensus, of cross-party agreement, as a kind of inevitable development where differences were about means rather than about ends. The political scientist Rudolf Klein argues that well before the wartime experience there was a general consensus about the need for a national health service. That consensus was the overarching framework within which debates about how the service was to be achieved took place during and after the war. This was what Klein calls the theme of 'conflict within consensus' which runs through the whole history of the NHS (Klein, 1995, p. 6). He posits a view of the NHS as the outcome of a kind of techno-bureaucratic consensus, with politicians, except at certain points, playing relatively small roles and outside groups, with the exception of the medical profession, having even slighter influence. Daniel Fox also focuses on consensus, but differs from other analysts in arguing that there were distinct similarities between the NHS and the form of health services established by other Western nations at this time. Fox categorises the dominant influence of what he calls 'hierarchic regionalism' as a common theme in Western health policy in the pre- and post-war period. 'Each country in Western Europe and North America has mandated or encouraged the creation of graded hierarchies of hospitals and physicians organised in geographic regions and has subsidised its citizens' access to these regional hierarchies' (Fox, 1986, p. 33).

Such stress upon collective provision, the pooling of risks, and strong popular endorsement is now questioned. The war was no 'golden age' of social solidarity. Evacuation, for example, reinforced rather than undermined class prejudices; perceptions of lice-ridden, bedwetting, poorly behaved children, visited by raucous and slovenly mothers, often intensified prejudices rather than removing them (MacNicol, 1986). A survey of public opinion in 1942 showed widespread and deep grievances against the existing system, but little coherent conception of what should take its place (Harris, 1983). Social solidarity was limited and the desire for radical change circumscribed. Nor was the vaunted political consensus a reality. Jefferys (1987) has argued that there were clear political differences between the Labour and Conservative Parties notably over the 1944 White Paper *A National Health Service*. The Conservatives focused mainly upon extension of pre-war services, Labour on more radical reform, with the two Parties as far apart on social policy in 1945 as they had been in 1939. The official historian of the health service, Charles Webster, taking the two issues of regionalism and of health centre development, has stressed conflict rather than consensus in the establishment of the health service. Organised labour, in his interpretation, emerges as a significant participant in events leading up to the formation of the service, with a coalition between labour and the senior civil service. Webster's view is that it is unrealistic to separate debates about means from those about ends. Both were inextricably interwoven (Webster, 1990). These debates are continuing and fresh discussion of the concept of consensus will undoubtedly emerge from further research. Evacuation may have led to more change than MacNicol allowed for; there was a major reassessment of the effectiveness of health services for schoolchildren. The war was a major watershed in the history of school medical provision (Harris, 1995; Welshman, 1998). It undoubtedly led to a determination to do something about the burden of poverty and ill health which had been revealed.

## War time events

Although the idea of consensus has been undermined by historical research on the wartime period, there is no doubt that a broad band of opinion was being converted even before the war to support some form of collective provision. This continued during the war. The BMA convened a Medical Planning Commission whose report in 1942 was supposed to represent the opinions of all medical groups (though its radical proposals proved unacceptable to BMA opinion and it was not pursued). But change came in the hospital sector. The overhaul and integration of hospital services had been widely recognised to be necessary on financial and other grounds. The King Edward's Hospital Fund for London had striven since the beginning of the century for greater efficiency in the use of the London hospitals. The Nuffield Provincial Hospitals Trust, founded in 1939, had as its primary aim the regional coordination of hospital services. Pressure from these organisations, the financial situation of the voluntary hospitals and the expected need to deal with large numbers of bombing casualties were what lay behind the establishment of the Emergency Hospital Service at the end of 1939. The hospitals were run by existing authorities, but within a regional framework and with the Ministry of Health deciding what role each should play.

A strong impetus to comprehensive proposals on the part of the

Ministry of Health came with the publication of the Beveridge Report in 1942 on *Social Insurance and Allied Services*. The significance of the report for wartime social policy should not be overstated. Its significance was less in the originality of the report's work than in its plans to rationalise the disjointed insurance schemes in existence before the war (Harris, 1981). The report's recommendation for a comprehensive social security system, based on subsistence rate benefits, assumed that among other benefits would be a national health service which would be free and comprehensive. Its immense public popularity gave a further impetus to discussions within the Ministry of Health and in February 1943, the government announced its acceptance of the principle of a free national health service, outlining a timetable for consultation and eventual legislation. The assumption behind this commitment, at least on the part of the Ministry of Health and the local authority associations, was that the new service would be established on the basis of the extension of local authority provision of services. The focus of the plan was general practice. GPs would lose their independent status and become salaried local authority employees. They would work in health centres which would bring them together with other local authority staff (Webster, 1998). The NHS White Paper of 1944 associated with Henry Willink, the Conservative MP who was the new Minister of Health, introduced a modified version. The White Paper was vague on several contentious issues; it was a consultative document and stressed that it wished to build on the pre-war structures of voluntarism, local authority control and health insurance.

Its publication revealed that one of the major planks of opposition to the idea of a national health service was the medical profession itself, or at least certain influential sections of it. Hospital consultants and GPs working in wealthy areas were opposed to a salaried service and local authority control, although Medical Officers of Health and GPs working in poorer areas gave it support. Months of negotiation between Willink and the BMA had led to substantial concessions on the government's part by 1945. The administrative role of local government was weakened at the expense of the professional organisations; there was new financial provision for the voluntary hospitals; and doctors in health centres would not be local salaried employees. A white paper on this basis was fully prepared, but was suppressed in June 1945 because of a possible adverse response from the electorate. Webster (1998) concludes that the substantial capitulation to medical and voluntary hospital interests had led to health service plans which offered the worst of all worlds, and failed to command support.

## *The impact of Bevan and of the Labour government*

It is the road *from* rather than the road *to* 1945 which is important, according to current historical analysis of the origins of the NHS. The achievements of the post-1945 Labour government and of Aneurin Bevan as Minister of Health were considerable. Bevan was determined to achieve a universal free service, but faced vehement opposition from the doctors, from sections of the Labour Cabinet, and also from the Conservative Party. Bevan's plan, which he put to the Cabinet in October and December 1945, contained the important policy departure of the nationalisation of the hospital system. All hospitals, whether voluntary or local authority, were to be coordinated by appointed local bodies with voluntary membership exercising powers delegated by central government. The twin proposals of nationalisation and regionalisation found favour with both Ministry of Health civil servants and with Lord Moran, one of the consultants' leaders. But this was a clear departure from Labour Party policy. Opposition within the Cabinet was led by Herbert Morrison, who, as leader of the London County Council, had responsibility for the largest public hospital system in Europe (Webster, 1988a and b). Morrison emphasised that the move from a rate- to a tax-based system would lead to an increase in expenditure. His experience of the LCC hospital system also made him oppose a system which removed democratic accountability and control. The subsequent history of the NHS has been bedevilled by this lack of popular participation. But Bevan had the majority in the Cabinet; the NHS Bill published in March 1946 proposed a service conducted through three main channels, hospital, GP and local authority services. Both voluntary and local hospitals were to be nationalised and placed under the control of regional boards consisting of local authority and voluntary representatives. The voluntary teaching hospitals were to be allowed considerable independence within this structure, retaining their own endowments and boards of governors. Consultants could be whole or part time; and private practice within the hospital was allowed as a more acceptable alternative to the proliferation of separate private institutional care. Counties and county boroughs kept responsibility for health centres, clinics and other services such as health visiting and ambulances. GP, dental and pharmacy services were to be administered by executive councils, half professional and half lay, with local authority and ministerial appointees. Health centres under local authority control were to be the linchpin of the system, and doctors were to be paid on a part salary part capitation fee basis. The possibility of a fully salaried service was dropped.

Opposition came from the Conservative Party during the second and third readings. The nationalisation of the voluntary hospitals and local authority controlled health centres were the particular focus. The Conservatives secured no real concessions and saddled themselves with an image of having opposed the Bill. But between the passing of the NHS Act in 1946 and the Appointed Day for the inauguration of the service on 5 July 1948, a number of concessions were forced out of the government. The new system was acceptable to consultants, in particular after the Spens Report (1948) on consultants' pay had held out the promise of a merit awards system, but GPs were unhappy with the new system. Important sections of the proposed service, such as the possibility of salaried service, were whittled away. Few health centres, the intended linchpin coordinating the system, were proposed or built.

The achievement of the Labour government elected in 1945 was considerable. Recent revision of uncritical earlier assessments of Bevan have nevertheless recognised his considerable achievement against determined professional opposition (Campbell, 1987). The nationalisation of the hospitals, although later widely criticised, was acknowledged, even by Willink, the Conservative MP who had been Health Minister, to be the only solution which effectively unified and coordinated hospital provision. Nationalisation and regionalisation were seen as the only means of securing equity in health provision and the resources to carry out this objective. Lowe credits Bevan with removing two commercial intrusions into health care which had been widely resented in the interwar period: the approved societies and the sale of GP practices. But trade union and friendly society insurance had been popular. Bevan abolished the system of contributory health insurance which was retained by every other Western country – despite the knowledge that insurance was less cost effective than state provision (Lowe, 1993, p. 173). The service was universal, comprehensive and free. Freedom from doctors' charges was an enormous relief for many. A doctor who qualified in the first week of the NHS recalled how he saw people who had not visited a doctor for years.[1] Nor were the services offered only the second rate. All were accessible and the aim was to 'universalise the best'. Working-class women who had limited access to services before gained especially from the NHS.

The structure established for the National Health Service perpetuated many of the anomalies and inequalities of the previous system. The tripartite system which had operated before 1939 carried over into the NHS (Lewis, 1992a). Major disadvantages were this fragmentation, the escalation of hospital costs and the lack of democratic accountability in all senses. The decision not to unify the services under local authority control ensured that the hospital sector would dominate and that costs would escalate. The regional hospital structure was effectively handed over to voluntary hospital interests. The expertise of the GP, excluded from hospital practice, initially declined under the NHS. Public health services, located in the local authorities, fared even worse. Medical Officers of Healths' control of municipal hospitals ended in 1948 and their clinical work declined because of the availability of GP services. Without adequate funding the health centres failed to develop and public health began a crisis of identity from which it has arguably yet to emerge. The alienation of the new discipline of social medicine from practical public health emphasised its decline (Lewis, 1986; Porter, 1997).

The failure to base health services on the local authorities has been seen by many commentators as a crucial 'wrong turning'. The NHS confirmed a system of health care where there was little popular participation. The insurance-based systems established in other countries at the same time may have been more expensive,

---

[1] Debate 7 January 1998 at the King's Fund on the past, present and future of the NHS at which the author was present. Speakers included Alan Langlands, the Chairman of the NHS Executive and Dr Julian Tudor Hart. Dr John Marks, formerly of the BMA, spoke about the origins of the NHS.

but they also gave greater influence to workers in maintaining the standard of the service. 'Club practice' in Britain at the end of the nineteenth century had had a similar effect, but the NHS was doctor dominated and the patient had little influence as an organiser or, in the phraseology of the 1990s, as a 'consumer' of health care. Women gained in terms of access to health care, although this improved access was also accompanied by treatments over which women, and other patients as well, had little control. Preventive medicine, widely discussed in the pre-war blueprints for health reform, was largely absent. Certainly public health, as then organised and conceptualised, did not fit this model. As more than one commentator remarked, the NHS was a national *sickness* service not a national *health* service. Behind the establishment of the service also lay the notion of a burden of ill health which would ultimately be reduced by free access to health care and the raising of standards of health. It soon became apparent in the post-war years that demands for health care were much wider and the issue of costs became a continuing theme. The organisational model adopted for the NHS ensured that this issue would be an intensely political one. Further reorganisations of the NHS from the 1970s to the 90s have increased the awareness of its serious structural inadequacies. But the undoubted achievements of the establishment of the NHS and the real gains which followed should not thereby be obscured.

## The impact of the war on health

The reorganisation of health services aside, what was the impact of the war on civilian health? Titmuss is again the starting point; his contention that the war had positive effects has received widespread support. The attainment of full employment after the unemployment of the 1930s did most to stabilise the working-class economy, helped by rent control, effective food rationing, the provision of free milk under the National Milk Scheme, and strict limitations on the production and distribution of alcohol. As in the First World War, there was a growing commitment by the state to defend the health of mothers and children. Factory creches, child and maternal welfare centres and nurseries were built and opened at a rapid rate during the war. By 1943, for the first time, a majority of pregnant women attended antenatal centres early in their pregnancy. By 1945, over 70% of the infants born in the previous year were brought to infant welfare centres (Winter, 1983).

But the evidence of infant mortality, a sensitive index of social conditions, divides the demographic history of the Second World War into two periods, 1939–42 and 1943–5. The first period is one of marked deterioration in infant survival chances; the second, one of substantial improvement. The period of improvement coincided with rising real wages through price control and increased opportunities for piece-work and overtime. This pattern of initial decline and subsequent improvement characterises the wartime period. Standards of living definitely rose towards the end of the war, unlike those in other European combatant countries, but the wartime experience of the civilian population was more equivocal than the unalloyed optimism of earlier accounts would allow.

Bombing and evacuation each produced their own strains. The earlier fears that more than 2 million beds would be needed for bombing casualties were not realised, but nevertheless, until D-Day in 1944, more civilians than soldiers died from enemy action. Incessant disruption of sleep led to chronic tiredness and the blackout induced both depression as the war dragged on, and also a rise in road accidents. Fears of the spread of venereal disease (VD), in particular after the arrival of American troops in Britain in 1942, lead to the passing of Defence Regulation 33B, which provided for compulsory examination and treatment of those suspected of having infected two or more persons with VD. In the same year a national publicity campaign was launched and local authority treatment centres increased in number in line with other municipal facilities (Davenport-Hines, 1990; Jones, 1994). Illegitimacy rates soared. Between 1940 and 1945, more than 300,000 illegitimate babies were born in England, Wales and Scotland, over 100,000 more than in the six years preceding the war. This, as Jones (1994) remarks, is an unreliable guide to sexual mores and their supposed loosening during the war. The apparent increase was caused by fewer women marrying when they discovered they were pregnant, and possibly also by the difficulties of contraception with the wartime shortage of rubber. The increased mobility of the population meant that it was easier to lose touch. The lot of the unmarried mother was, however, still harsh and unmarried women were subjected to widespread social disapproval.

Women, supposedly assisted by better provision of child care and maternity facilities, experienced the equivocal health effects of the war. Bearing the dual burden of domestic and war work, women were still seen primarily as wives and mothers and the war did not necessarily produce more defined career paths for them (Summerfield, 1984). Within the family economy, rationing, introduced in 1940, bore more heavily on women, who had traditionally 'gone short' so that other members of the family could benefit.

Most evidence suggests that health improved towards the end of the war, closely linked to rising standards of living. From 1941, there were price controls, full employment and food rationing, with the basics available to most people, and supplements to the diets of particular groups such as pregnant women and young children. Cheap meals were provided through school meals, works' canteens and British Restaurants, cheap state-run restaurants. The contribution of better nutrition to improved health standards was widely recognised, although social class inequalities remained striking, reflected in subsequent information on body height and weight (Oddy, 1982).

Such advances were achieved with lower inputs from formal medical care. As in the First World War, civilians had a much diminished chance of seeing a doctor during the war because doctors were absent on military service. Some of the gap was filled by the use of patent medicines, which was widespread and by 'counter prescribing' by pharmacists. But more seriously ill people were undoubtedly disadvantaged during the war. So, too, were old people, many of whom were among the chronically sick discharged from hospitals at the beginning of the war in the expectation of bombing casualties. Although establishment of a subsistence pension was part of Beveridge's recommendations, he did not give this section of the population high priority (McNicol and Blaikie, in Jefferys, 1989). The main pensioner campaigning organisation focused on pensions issues rather than inadequacies in medical and social provision. War time discussions certainly contributed to the linking of retirement to state support for the elderly and to the gradual emergence of the ageing issue as a post-war 'social problem'. Thane (1990) has pointed out that the 'problem' of the elderly was an issue for the interwar years as well.

The beginnings of other post-war developments can also be discerned during the war. Health education, a cornerstone of subsequent health policy, was supported through the Central Council for Health Education (CCHE), originally founded in 1927 by the Society of Medical Officers of Health. Treasury support for VD education went to that Council during the war; it subsumed the earlier British Social Hygiene Council in 1942. Health education took on a wider role in the context of war and work discipline, with health education displays in cinema foyers in the 1940s and work place campaigns aimed at both workers and management (Blythe, 1986; Jones, 1994). Similar campaigns in the army emphasised self-discipline as the key to good hygiene.[2] Psychological approaches were stimulated through the needs of the war effort. Group therapy, first started among ex-servicemen, was established in the mental health services, and there was a greater emphasis on child guidance and psychology as well.

Wartime advances in medical science were less apparent to the civilian population and their benefits only featured afterwards. Penicillin, developed at Oxford during the war, was commercially exploited in America, its benefits initially restricted to the military (Weatherall, 1993). The Blood Transfusion and Public Health Laboratory Services, regionally organised because of the wartime emergency, were initially of limited use to the civilian population (Oakley and Ashton, 1997; Williams, 1985).

Fifty years on, the assessment of the development of health services, and of the impact of the war on civilian health, must be mixed. Older 'golden age' interpretations, which emphasised social and political consensus and the march of welfare and health reform, are viewed more critically in contemporary scholarship. The war was not an unequivocal benefit for civilian health. There was co-existence between different forms of provision. Voluntary activity, for example, expanded during the war at the same time as the role of the state increased (Finlayson, 1994). Inequalities in health persisted alongside the undoubted rise in health status towards the end of

[2] M. Harrison, talk at Leicester Health Education conference, 1995, unpublished.

the war. But high hopes at the end of the war were accompanied by optimistic assumptions that the health of the nation and its health services could be further improved. How these beliefs translated into practice will be discussed in the following chapter.

## 3
# Health policy, health and society, 1948–1974

## The organisation of services

The establishment of the National Health Service was part of moves across Western Europe and Australasia in the period 1945–64 to extend the role of the state in the provision of health care. Most systems were based on compulsory social insurance with direct links between payments and benefits and a higher degree of bureaucracy and decentralisation. In France, payment was on a fee for service basis through a mixture of social security and insurance benefits. In the United States, a large proportion of the population was privately insured, with inadequate reimbursement for some of the remainder (Baggott, 1994). Suggestions that British post-war welfare policy drained resources away from the modernisation of industry and technology underplayed the extent to which these developments were a Western European rather than a peculiarly British phenomenon (Barnett, 1986). However, the principles of unconditional relief of poverty and equality of access were more strongly built into the British health system than elsewhere. The British system was also unusual in being centrally funded out of taxation, which helped to secure the political ideal of a free and equal service for all to a degree unmatched in other Western European countries. Nevertheless, the NHS also had its structural and financial deficiencies from the outset, as discussed in the previous chapter. The circumstances of the service's inception and the various strategies adopted to secure the support of the medical profession ensured that decisions had been taken which led directly to some of its later problems. Financial and structural issues, together with broader demographic and technological change and rising public expectations, all served to create problems in the post-war period. These problems gathered pace from the 1970s, but this section will discuss how these concerns also began to affect the NHS from its earliest days.

## The issue of costs

Finance was chief among these. Early planning of the NHS had assumed that costs might eventually fall once the backlog of untreated illness was met. There was indeed a huge increase in the supply of dentures, spectacles and hearing aids. Provisional estimates for the service in 1949/50 showed costs expanding unevenly – 24% for non-teaching hospitals, but 320% for dentists and 460% for opticians (Webster, 1988, pp.137–8). Pay review boards also awarded pay rises well above the rate of inflation. It soon became obvious that the cost of the service would be a continuing political issue as the initial costs of the service were well above estimated expenditure (Webster 1988a, table opposite p. 134). Some contemporary critics such as Ffrangcon Roberts argued that the demand for health care was actually infinite and held out the prospect of totalitarianism as the end of the welfare state (Roberts, 1952).

Yet costs were not out of control; and misconceptions on this issue have bedevilled subsequent discussion of NHS funding as Webster has shown. During its first decade, the current net cost of the NHS averaged about 3.5% of gross domestic product (GDP), supplanting expenditure of between 3.0 and 3.5% of GDP in the immediate pre- and post-war periods. Post-war Labour and Conservative governments were so successful in holding down the costs of health care that expenditure on the health service as a proportion of GNP actually fell in the early 1950s. It was not until the later 1950s and 60s that the service's overall share of the national budget began to rise. Even so, by the early 1970s, Britain's expenditure on health care as a percentage of GDP was, at 4.1%, lower than most other Western European countries, with the exception of Spain, Switzerland, Greece, Belgium and Norway.[1] Webster's study of the

---

[1] J. Hutton, 'The costs of health care; an historical and economic perspective', unpublished paper, 1995.

fluctuations in NHS growth under different administrations during this period shows how a consensus emerged between the health department and the Treasury that an annual growth rate of 2.5% was 'about right'; this fluctuated over time. Growth and relative decline appear to have been largely unrelated to the political complexion of particular administrations and more to external factors such as devaluation in 1969 and the oil crisis in the 1970s. The rigid resource constraints established during the first decade of the service established norms against which the NHS has been measured ever since.

This was not the perception at the time. NHS costs seemed wildly out of control, and the Ministry of Health was unable to predict the cost of short-term need or to provide a basis for future expenditure decisions. Battles over costs occupied the attention of the post-war Labour government. Prescription charges were proposed in 1949 (but imposed subsequently by the new Conservative government), together with a ceiling on expenditure. A special Cabinet Committee monitored NHS expenditure and how it could be limited. In 1951 the Chancellor, Hugh Gaitskell's announcement of charges for dentistry and the optician service led to the resignation of Bevan, John Freeman and Harold Wilson from the Cabinet.

The Guillebaud Committee, announced in April 1952 by the new Conservative Minister of Health, Ian Macleod, was to examine 'the present and prospective cost of the NHS'. It was intended as the prelude to cost cutting, but in fact concluded that the opposite was needed. Its findings were largely based on a pioneering research report from two LSE academics, Brian Abel-Smith and Richard Titmuss, which for the first time related health expenditure to inflation and economic growth. It concluded that it would be premature to introduce change to the NHS. Taking into account demographic change and inflation, the cost per head at constant prices was almost the same in 1953/4 as it had been in 1949/50. Capital investment was proportionally lower than it had been in the 1930s for hospitals. The report in fact recommended increased spending and proposed a seven-year annual programme of £30m from 1957/8. A bitter disappointment to the government, it nevertheless underlined the relative cost-effectiveness of the NHS, even if some have criticised the report for its failure to think constructively about alternative options. John Brotherston attacked the Committee for standing 'hypnotized in front of the status quo' (quoted in Fox, 1986, p. 181).

## A post-war consensus?

The notion of 'wartime consensus' has been criticised. The Guillebaud Committee's appointment by a Conservative government might lend some credence to the idea of post-war consensus about the nature and objectives of the NHS. This view of the first post-war Conservative administration (Klein, 1995) has been questioned in recent years. Webster (1994) has argued that the government's priority was to minimise expenditure on the NHS. A second line of attack was to institute cuts and to find alternatives to funding from central taxation. The campaign for economies found an ally in the early 1960s when Enoch Powell became Minister of Health. He, like the Treasury, favoured increased charges for dental and ophthalmic services and a doubling of the prescription charge. Harriet Jones' research has shown that the Conservative government was consistently concerned about the impact of increased welfare expenditure on economic performance, but the government elected in 1951 was unable to reverse the Attlee government's spending patterns. Ian Macleod and Enoch Powell had an important role in the Conservative Research Department aiming to reorientate the welfare state to a system based on need. For the NHS, they suggested charges together with an expanded role for the private sector for those able to pay for care. But political realities dictated that none of this became practical policy. Conservative health policy was the product of the tension between what was ideologically and economically desirable and what was politically feasible (Jones, 1991, 1992). Timmins' conclusion that there was 'consensus in action', if not in underlying ideology, is perhaps an appropriate one (Timmins, 1995).

The Guillebaud Report had urged that increased resources be put towards modernising the creaking facilities of the NHS. The expanding economy of the late 1950s and 1960s enabled finance to be directed towards health without controversy. It remained, as at its inception, overwhelmingly a tax-funded system. Popular belief had it that contributions covered the full cost (a misconception still alive in the 1990s when whittling away the principle of universalism was attacked on the basis that contributors had 'paid in' for a full range of services). Conservatives, too, seriously considered a move to an insurance funded-system. The proposal was reluctantly dropped although the contribution of the insurance fund to the NHS did increase in the late 1950s and early 1960s (see Lowe, 1993, table 7.3, p. 183). Consideration of alternatives to taxation continued, reviving with particular force at the onset of the 1970–4 Conservative government. The increased influence of the Institute for Economic Affairs with the Secretary of State, Sir Keith Joseph, brought consideration, against Treasury opposition, of insurance-based alternatives, but to little effect. Tinkering with prescription charges and involvement with Public Expenditure Survey Committee (PESC) annual reviews remained other options for raising finance (Webster, 1996).

## Hospitals and high technology

Central Treasury direction apart, government and the Ministry of Health had relatively little control over the operation of many parts of the service, in particular those under the local authorities. This tension between local self-determination and central policy making remained an enduring issue within the NHS. Benner draws attention to the doctrine of local managerial responsibility and what he calls the 'managerial vacuum' at the centre (Benner, 1989). Edwards (1995), in a managerial study of the history of the NHS, also highlights the ambiguity in lines of management in the early years of the service. The authority of regions over hospital management committees remained unclear. But the hospitals, which were under state control, did offer the opportunity for planned expansion and increased allocation of resources. The 1962 Hospital Plan, originating under Derek Walker-Smith as Minister of Health, but always associated with his successor, Enoch Powell (and strongly favoured by the redoubtable Chief Medical Officer (CMO), Sir George Godber), aimed to guarantee access for the medical profession and the public to the most technologically modern facilities. It envisaged that over the next decade work would start on building 90 new hospitals and substantially remodelling 134 others. National norms for beds were laid down (e.g. 3.3. acute beds per 1,000 population).

The aim was to create a national pattern of District General Hospitals of 600–800 beds each serving a population of 100,000–150,000, figures which were doubled by the end of the decade. Between the late 1940s and the mid-1960s, hospitals enjoyed a 13% increase in resources at the expense of general medical, dental and ophthalmic services (Webster, 1993, p. 111).

This was, as Klein remarks, 'the child of a marriage between professional aspirations and the new faith in planning: between what might be called medical expertise and administrative technology' (Klein, 1995, p.67). The professional definition of the problem was paramount. The acute hospital sector and its increasing technological sophistication dominated. The aim, as Webster has commented, was to bring within the reach of all X-ray and pathological laboratory facilities, a comprehensive blood transfusion service, proper accident and emergency facilities. The main problem was that neither the health departments nor the NHS authorities had reached settled conclusions about the scope and character of the modern hospital system to which they were aspiring. The district general hospital emerged as the approved objective, but without being particularly well worked out (Webster, 1996, p. 105).

It later became fashionable to decry high technology medicine because of its high cost and distorting effect on the pattern of services. The faith in 'high tech' medicine was at its peak in this period; new technologies such as renal dialysis and transplantation offered fresh possibilities and new specialities proliferated (Rivett, 1998). Neurosurgery, thoracic surgery and plastic surgery, formerly established in a few centres, were provided in every region. Pathology and anaesthesia established large specialist cadres (Beinart, 1987). Support services such as radiography and blood transfusion expanded. Between 1948 and 1958, the number of bottles of blood issued more than doubled in England and Wales and more than trebled in Scotland (Webster, 1996, pp. 17–18). Lawrence (1994) provides an introduction to the socio-political context of technological advance. The example of renal dialysis shows how rationing of an expensive technology, although not yet on the political agenda in the 1960s and 70s, was none the less operating covertly and in a paternalistic way through the control exercised by doctors (Stanton, 1999).

The NHS had at its inception been a hospital-focused service. Although the demand for hospital services in some areas declined (as, for example, the decline of tuberculosis led to the reallocation of TB beds in isolation hospitals), developments in other areas brought fresh demands. Nowhere was this subsequently more contentious than in the hospitalization of childbirth. The rise of obstetrics and gynaecology was accompanied by better access to medical services but also increasingly sophisticated treatments over which women had little control. By 1944, the Royal College of Obstetricians and Gynaecologists was aiming for 70% of births to be hospital based and this became a self-fulfilling prophecy in the post-war years. Childbirth in hospital increased from approximately 50 to 96% of all births between the mid-1940s and the 1970s. Subsequent feminist criticism of the technological and professional domination of these services has tended to underestimate the demand for hospital childbirth from working-class women. Given poor housing conditions and high levels of maternal mortality, there was much to be said for childbirth in hospital, in particular because of the access which it gave to pain relief. In the 1930s, 'twilight sleep' during childbirth and general anaesthesia during delivery were available to middle-class women, but not to working-class women giving birth at home; the demand for these services has to be recognised. The NHS was at its inception, and has remained, a service with immense popularity and the 'medical model' retains popular support. Bevan, it was said, derived his faith in hospital medicine from his experience of general practice in Tredegar.[2] His remark that he would rather survive in the cold but efficient altruism of a large hospital than expire in a gush of warm sympathy in a small one (Lowe, 1993, p. 184) found its echo in the hospital-focused policies of this period.

## *Science, drugs and the pharmaceutical industry*

The formal health care system was dominated by the 'medical model' which set in place an implicit set of assumptions about the role of medical science. Advances in post-war medical science ap-

---

[2] Debate 7 January 1998 at the King's Fund on the past, present and future of the NHS (see p. 17 n. 1).

peared to confirm this view. Trials of streptomycin for TB funded by the Medical Research Council (MRC) in 1946 established both its efficacy but also began the long post-war rise of the controlled clinical trial. In the 1950s the results of the 1950 BCG trial were published (Bryder, 1999). The effect of penicillin, the sulphonamides and other drugs had begun this therapeutic revolution in the decade before the establishment of the NHS and the post-war period saw a further expansion in the production of new and effective drugs and therapies. Antibiotics and psychotropic drugs for the control of mental illness were among them. Webster (1996, p. 13) notes that by 1958, antibiotics and hormones accounted for 20% and 8% respectively of the drug bill whereas they had been negligible factors ten years earlier. Possibilities of the conquest of disease added to the therapeutic optimism of this period.

These therapeutic advances also brought problems in their train. The thalidomide tragedy of 1958–61 led to greater controls over the licensing of new pharmaceutical products through the establishment of the Committee on the Safety of Drugs (CSD) in 1963 (Abraham, 1995; Watkin, 1978). That committee worked on the basis of voluntary regulation of the industry, and this approach carried over subsequently into the establishment of the Medicines Commission in 1968 and the transmutation of the CSD into the Committee on the Safety of Medicines. The establishment of these regulatory frameworks gave an enormous boost to the clinical trials industry which thereafter spread into other areas of medical research as the 'gold standard' of objectivity. The voluntary approach was one which government had already adopted in its negotiations over the price of drugs used in the service. Voluntary price regulation agreements operated for much of this period. However, in the 1970s, the government did refer Roche products to the Monopolies Commission because of the level of tranquilliser prices.

## Mental health

The Hospital Plan was a monument to the technological vision of the 1960s. But some hospitals in the service remained neglected and underfunded. The large Victorian asylums remained separately administered from the rest of the service established in 1948. But here too technical advance brought change. The arrival of new drug therapies in the 1950s offered the possibility of release into the community of many asylum inhabitants. Jones (1993) notes that three 'revolutions' were under way in the mental health field in the 1950s. As well as the pharmacological revolution, there were also social and administrative changes and change in the legal system relating to mental illness. Administrative change saw the institution of 'open door' policies, leading to a range of options including therapeutic communities and day hospitals. Legal change was brought about by the Royal Commission on Mental Illness and Mental Deficiency, which had the 1959 Mental Health Act as its outcome. The Act enshrined the liberalisation of attitudes to mental illness (the term which replaced madness and lunacy), brought the mental health system under the local health authorities, and contained important steps towards community care (Unsworth, 1987). The move towards community care was carried further through the Hospital Plan, which envisaged cutting psychiatric beds by half. Jones sees opposition to this move as muted in part because of the increasing acceptance of new theoretical analyses of mental health, emanating from the social and political theorists Goffman, Foucault and Szasz, and with British counterparts in R. D. Laing and others. From differing theoretical traditions, they criticised the professional and institutional control of mental illness (Jones, 1993, pp. 165–78). But the release of patients from these institutions and from others catering for mental handicap and for the elderly was delayed. Scandals about the state of the long stay institutions came to public attention in the late 1960s. Richard Crossman as DHSS Minister in 1969 found that there were a quarter of a million people in long stay, subnormal, psychiatric and geriatric hospitals. His insistence on the full publication of the report on scandals in patient care at the Ely Hospital in Cardiff brought an independent hospital inspectorate reporting to the Minister (Crossman, 1979, pp. 591–4). The scandals were paralleled by the deficiencies of long-term care for the elderly, exposed by Peter Townsend in *The Last Refuge*. These developments are further discussed in the following section on community care. However, not all areas within mental health were focused on community care. Alcohol treatment took up the hospital option after a 1962 memorandum on the subject; and the treatment of drug abuse was also located within hospitals under psychiatric control by the end of the 1960s (Thom and Berridge, 1995). British psychiatry flourished institutionally through the research-based Institute of Psychiatry led by the charismatic figure of Aubrey Lewis.

## Reorganisation of the NHS: first attempt, 1968–1974

The fragmentation of the service remained a major deficiency. Health centres, intended originally to be the coordinating linchpin of the new service, were not developed in its early years. By 1963, only eighteen health centres had been purpose built in England and Wales, as a reflection of limitations on capital expenditure, practical problems over sites and planning and the reluctance of GPs (Hall, 1986 reprint). Increasingly reorganisation to promote coordination joined expenditure levels as a focus of policy concern. In England and Wales there were more than 400 hospital authorities and a total of about 700 administrative authorities involved in the health service. In some respects, coordination of the service had been greater before the NHS than after, especially within the larger local authorities. Pressure for change came from two directions, from the medical profession and from the Ministry of Health. The profession wanted a clearer 'high tech' role for the hospital and better coordination in terms of prevention and after care with general practice, developing its new post-war role (as discussed below in the third section, pp. 41–3) and with local authority services. The Ministry wanted appropriate administrative machinery so that its policies could be implemented. The belief in the 'organisational fix' was paramount: the NHS was trying to solve its problems through tinkering with the organisation of the service (Klein, 1995, p. 82; Allsop, 1995b).

There were, as in the 1940s, two possibilities for reorganisation; through local government and through expanded hospital authorities. Achieving any reorganisation at all became a Byzantine procedure which lasted ultimately for over six years and took the attention of both the Labour government and its Conservative successor. Webster (1996) is critical of the Labour Minister of Health, Kenneth Robinson, for failing to take the initiative when the issue was in its early stages. Although reform of local government was in train, this arrangement was unacceptable to the medical profession, and so as in 1948, the hospital option was chosen. The initial restructuring proposed that there should be forty to fifty Area Health Authorities, each responsible for the full range of health services in its area, and geographically similar to the reorganised major local authorities. Delay and a change of government from Labour to Conservative wrought significant changes in this plan. Local government reform also took a different form to that expected at the time of the first Labour Green Paper in 1968. When reorganisation took effect in 1974, the final blueprint bore little relationship to the original design. The Area Health Authorities were coterminous with the new local government units responsible for social services. Above them, responsible for planning, were 14 Regional Health Authorities, and below were 205 District Management Teams. Care was not unified. Family practitioner committees (updated Executive Councils) were excluded from the remit of the AHAs. Although coterminous with them, they were largely autonomous. Membership of the AHAs drew in equal proportion from nominees of local government, the medical profession and the state. The role of the consumer was recognised for the first time through the establishment of Community Health Councils, which shadowed the work of the District Management Teams. The local authorities remained to one side, apparently losing responsibility for health services but in fact retaining important health related areas such as environmental health and community care.

Virtually the only element of greater coordination was the abolition of the independent status of the prestigious teaching hospitals. The new NHS was criticised as being excessively managerialist, but now provided three layers of administration instead of the original one while the doctrine of 'consensus management' through District Management Teams was a recipe for further delay. Ideas promoted during Sir Keith Joseph's tenure as Secretary of State, of an NHS chief executive, of the service run by a separate corporation, and of general rather than consensus management, did not win acceptance at the time, but were revived as apparently new initiatives in the 1980s (Webster, 1996, chapter VI and p. 742). 'The paradoxical consequence of the 1974 reorganisation exercise', writes Webster, 'was a service more bureaucratically complex and only marginally more unified than the organisation hastily contrived by the Labour government in 1945' (Webster, 1993, p. 130).

## Community care and lay care

Although hospital-based technocratic medicine dominated health services, another policy objective was to remove sections of institutional populations into what became known as 'community care'. Much used in the 1980s and 90s, this term first appeared in 1950s policy documents; it expressed a broad policy objective for most post-war governments. But its meaning has been imprecise, encompassing care in residential homes as well as care provided at home. A shift in policy from care *in* the community to care *by* the community also occurred in the 1970s and 80s. Further, community care has become identified with the closure of long stay hospitals for the mentally ill and handicapped, thereby promoting controversy about a lack of adequate replacement facilities.

Community care can also be defined in relation to the form of provision. Broadly, it can be provided by formal health and social services; through the voluntary sector; and informally through friends, neighbours and family. In the 1980s and 90s, there has been much emphasis on the 'mixed economy' of care in which a range of providers of care can be utilised; here the role of the commercial sector has assumed a revived importance. There has been constant intermixing between the different sectors, with a series of shifting and interdependent relationships. In all these changes of emphasis the role of women as 'natural carers' has been significant (Hunter, 1993). Caring, as discussed below (pp. 71–2) is often by older people for older people.

### *Community care and the changing structure of the population*

One stimulus to the post-war development of community care was the changing age structure of the population discussed in chapter 1. Both maternal and infant mortality were in long-term decline. Loudon has emphasised that the reduction of maternal mortality was the result of the arrival of penicillin, the sulphonamides and the availability of blood transfusion as well as of improvements in general health. The decline of neonatal mortality is less easy to explain (Loudon, 1988, 1991). But the change which had greatest impact on community care was the significant growth in the proportion of old people in the population, due as much to the falling birth rate as to falling mortality. The elderly, along with infants, experienced the most striking falls in mortality. Over the period 1901–5 to 1961–5, mortality rates for females aged 75–84 fell by 22% and for males in the same age bracket by 14%. These trends continued and intensified in the period between the 1960s and the 1980s. The greatest rate of change had come in the period between 1901 and 1951, but the impact of those changes was perceived in the post-war period. The most significant change was the increase in the proportion of the very old. Numbers of over 80s increased fourfold between 1951 and 1989, doubling as a proportion of the over 65s from 12.7% in 1951 to 23% in 1989 (Tinker, 1994).

These changes led to much discussion of the role of old people in society and the burden which their increasing numbers was likely to pose. In the 1980s, commentators wrote of the 'structured dependency' of the elderly, the view that the economic dependency of old people had been socially manufactured in the post-war period in order to facilitate the removal of older workers from the labour market. The analysis, as Thane has pointed out, rests on the belief that the organisation of the modern economy and forms of state policies are the primary reason for the poverty, dependency and low social esteem of the elderly (Thane, 1989). Other historians pointed out that the 'structured dependency' argument rested on ahistorical assumptions about the nature of old age in the past. Thomson (1986), for example, argued that payments to pensioners under the Poor Law were more generous in relative terms before the 1870s than state pensions after 1946. The break in the continuity of publicly funded support for the elderly came in the 1870s when the state sought to shift responsibility to charitable institutions and to the family, a situation remedied only by the introduction of state pensions for the elderly in 1908. His arguments were not uncritically accepted, but the overall picture is one of constant shifts in relationship and the balance of provision over the past three centuries between central and local government, charity, family and other forms of informal support. Just as responsibility for the dependent aged was redefined in the later nineteenth century, so it was again following the Second World War. It was not that at either time dependence was newly structured, or even reinforced, but rather, that it was perpetuated (Thane 1989).

This restructuring, and the changing proportion of the very old, had implications for the provision of health and social care. The 'domiciliary care' of the elderly became an objective of policy just after the war; by 1956, the Deputy CMO, George Godber, could declare that 'no geriatric service can be really effective unless it is run as a safety valve for a service mainly of home care' (quoted in Webster, 1991, p. 172). The elderly were the perceived 'crisis group' of the 1950s; they appeared to be the only group still suffering poverty in the welfare state (Thane, 1990). A rash of investigations in the mid-1950s highlighted their needs and favoured the extension of community care, in part to resolve the problem of the growth of numbers of long stay elderly patients in NHS hospitals (Webster, 1991, p. 174). Geriatrics was also beginning to establish itself as a speciality in this period (Thane, 1993; Martin, 1995). The 1963 Health and Welfare White Paper on community care paralleled the 1962 Hospital Plan which had required the extension of community care in order to reduce the inpatient population. It was also a significant part of the Royal Commission on Mental Illness and the subsequent 1959 Act, discussed in the first section (pp. 30–2). The growing proportion of elderly in long stay mental hospitals was one means whereby the ageing problem presented itself. The percentage of over 65s in mental hospitals rose from 16. 4% to 20.0% between 1944 and 1954. Moving patients out of the mental hospitals and into the community became a high priority. The historian Andrew Scull argued that community care for mental health was primarily an economy measure, a strategy to avert a financial crisis of underfunding and overcrowding. But the international picture indicated that there was no automatic relationship between financial problems and the move towards community care (Jones, 1994; Scull, 1989; Unsworth, 1987). Powell as Health Minister was fully aware that community care had to be developed in tandem with the reduction of hospital beds in order to prevent the escalation of hospital costs (Webster, 1996, p. 124). The idea of domiciliary teams, comprising a range of different skills–home helps, health visitors, the general practitioner – was at the heart of the community care arrangements. Local authority staff in these categories did increase in the post-war period, and gradually their work became oriented towards the care of the elderly; the main defect was their small scale.

'Community care' of the elderly also encompassed residential care and former local authority institutional care became the health authority's community care (Walker quoted in Lewis, 1992a, p. 149). By 1960, local authority residential homes housed 84,000 old persons, including 39,000 in homes opened since 1948. But resources were directed towards long stay hospital accommodation and treatment and towards 'homes' which perpetuated the defects of the old workhouses (Townsend, 1962). Local authority plans produced in response to the Health and Welfare Report showed a projected rise of 87% for residential staff compared with only 45% for home helps (quoted in Lewis, 1992a, p. 149). Other academics were cautious even at this stage about the whole concept as a cheaper alternative to hospital care. Titmuss pointed out in 1961 that good community care was not cheap (quoted in Lewis, 1992a, p. 148). It was notable, too, that resources did not shift from health to local authority budgets to pay for community care in this period.

Community care continued as a policy objective both for the elderly and for the mentally ill in the 1970s. The scandals in the long stay hospitals in the 1960s already referred to, together with historical and sociological criticism of the asylum, discussed in the next chapter (pp. 56–7), brought further moves towards community care in the 1970s. Two White Papers, *Better Services for the Mentally Handicapped* (1971) and *Better Services for the Mentally Ill* (1975), developed a blueprint for community care. But in general the idea of community care did not receive further impetus until the election of the Thatcher government in 1979 and the resource imbalance for local authorities continued.

## The role of voluntarism

Although the establishment of state provision in health care continues to be the dominant historiographical theme in this period, recent historical work has drawn attention to the greater interdependence of relationships between the state and other forms of provision, doubtless in its turn influenced by the reduction of state provision and the revival of other forms of care in the 1980s and 90s. Both Prochaska and Finlayson have emphasised what William Beveridge called the 'moving frontier' of relationships with the voluntary sector (Finlayson, 1994; Prochaska, 1988). Voluntarism, once thought to have been eclipsed by the arrival of the welfare state, was a continuing strand. Reports in the 1950s and 1960s, for example the Younghusband report on social workers in 1959, placed emphasis on its role. Through meals on wheels, the hospital care service and hospital Leagues of Friends, it retained a presence in post-war health care. The Victorian Charity Organisation Society metamorphosed after 1946 into the Family Welfare Association.

This was the traditional 'helping' role of voluntarism. But the concept also underwent a change in the 1960s, with support from both ends of the political spectrum. The Conservatives favoured philanthropic charity to deliver more cost-effective services and to revive 'active' citizenship. Labour favoured a revival of mutual aid, and self-help and pressure groups sought to extend and redefine citizens' rights. The notion of participation gave further impetus to the voluntary sector in the 1960s and 1970s, with the rise of groups catering for those relatively neglected by the welfare state. Among such were the Spinal Injuries Association (1974), Help the Aged (1961), and the drugs legal charity Release (1967). A survey in 1978 found 40% of the organisations it covered had come into existence in the previous eight years, with special handicaps and diseases one of the fastest-growing areas (Finlayson, 1994, pp. 327–8).

Consumerism was an important force among pressure groups in general in the 1960s and 1970s, and the origins of consumerism in health care can also be traced to these decades. Amongst the earliest organisations pressing for more of a consumer 'say' were AIMS (Association for Improvements in Maternity Services), the National Association for the Welfare of Children in Hospital founded in 1961 and the Patients' Association. There also were improvements in hospital complaints procedures (Watkin, 1978, p. 122). Further developments in consumerism were presaged by the establishment of the Community Health Councils as part of the 1974 reorganisation. But the sociologist, Margaret Stacey, who had been an early advocate of consumerism in health, later expressed reservations

(Stacey, 1976). In her view, the differences of interest between doctor and patient, although real, were not of a producer-consumer nature. Some consumer and voluntary pressure groups operated in close relationship with the statutory sector, and could not have remained in existence without financial support from the state. The pressure group ASH (Action on Smoking and Health) was one example. Founded in 1971 in the wake of the second Royal College of Physicians report on smoking, it was primarily funded by the Department of Health (Berridge, 1998). This was one pattern of funding, but charities also raised large sums for research and patient care through their own activities.

The interrelationship of sectors, and the different sectors within statutory care, meant that coordination between services became a dominant policy theme. The 1974 planning system in theory provided a basis for cooperation with Joint Consultative Committees. There was a steady increase in staff in community-based services in this period, with a particularly sharp increase between 1967 and 1971. But it is not known whether these increases kept pace with demographic and social change. Almost twice as many pensioners lived alone in 1971 than had in 1961, although, as will be discussed below, the role of the family remained important as the focus of care (Allsop, 1995b, p. 98). As Allsop comments, 'like many other aspects of health and social care, it was easier to obtain measures of service inputs than outputs'.

*Informal care and community care*

Community care also encompassed informal care provided by family and neighbours. In the 1950s, studies such as the classic *Family and Kinship in East London* provided evidence of the continuity of patterns of family involvement in care, in particular in childbirth and child health (Young and Willmott, 1957). These patterns of informal care continued, as the accounts in Elizabeth Roberts' oral history study in the north of England demonstrate (Roberts, 1995). Not every historian supports the idea of a 'golden age'. Bourke has disputed the whole idea of working class community, arguing that the low spatial mobility and high population density in poor areas did not necessarily add up to a close knit community, which she sees as essentially a mythologised term (Bourke, 1994, p. 137). Relationships were likely to be more diverse and complex, not so radically altered by the move to new estates as some commentators have argued. Cornwell's interviews also cast doubt on the contrasts which Young and Willmott drew between life in the East End and the apparently more materially focused and atomised existence on the new housing estates. Those authors were more willing to acknowledge, and condemn, acquisitiveness in Greenleigh than in Bethnal Green. The private accounts she collected stressed the overriding importance of looking after oneself and one's own (Cornwell, 1984, pp. 43–8). What emerges from these different analyses is a greater sense of the complexity of family interaction. Although many old people lived alone, most had family or friends on whom they could count when needed. Mutual caring did continue in this period, although there was – and had always been – little that was cosy or romantic about it.

Roberts' research has found that the form of caring in relation to health issues changed as did the cultural context within which it took place. Activities such as the laying out of the dead became undertakers' rather than neighbours' work, while professional help, especially that of the doctor and health visitor, was increasingly sought and preferred to that of the older women in the family and neighbourhood. Getting the 'proper thing' from the doctor was preferred. Visits to the clinic increased, for their social as well as their medical value. Between 1940 and 1970 there was a noticeable shift from reliance on one's own judgement, and that of relations and neighbours with some support from experts, to a strong dependence on professionals with a corresponding diminution of self-reliance and self-confidence, certainly as far as child rearing was concerned (Roberts, 1995, p. 149). More general changes in women's role such as the increase in paid employment for women, and in the divorce and illegitimacy rates, which are discussed below, also had an impact. However, the effect of these changes should not be overstressed. Most working women continued in regular contact with their mothers. Help in bereavement, running errands to the chemists for prescriptions, sitting with the sick and other similar activities still continued.

So, too, did self-medication. A study in the 1950s of a working-class estate found that two-thirds of the people interviewed were taking some form of self-prescribed medicine, often in addition to a prescribed drug. Laxatives and aspirins were most commonly self-prescribed. The same was the case at the end of the 1960s. A major study by Karen Dunnell and Ann Cartwright found that 80% of a large sample of the population taken from across the country had taken some medicine in the two weeks prior to the interview. Again, it was self-prescribed medicines – aspirin, skin tonics and antacids – which outnumbered those prescribed by doctors by two to one (quoted in Helman, 1990, pp. 72–3). Self-medication and patterns of caring can also be related to the continuance of distinct lay beliefs about illness and disease. These are less amenable to chronological division – and are discussed in the fourth section of chapter 4 (p. 74–6).

## The health care division of labour

The growing emphasis on care in the community had consequences for the role and function of health care occupations. General practice benefited, redefining its role to encompass a much stronger community dimension, ironically at the expense of the Medical Officer of Health who lost status and influence at the local level.

### *The post-war rise of the general practitioner*

The status of general practice was at a low ebb at the inception of the NHS. General practitioners had begun to be excluded from hospitals in the interwar years, and the NHS further excluded them by forcing a choice between a hospital or a GP career. Access to the new laboratory-based specialist diagnostic techniques remained under the control of hospital specialists, and GPs were not allowed to use them until the 1950s or 1960s. Before the war the GPs function had been seen as 'cure', and had been closely related to hospital medicine (Armstrong, 1983). After the war, there was discontent with what seemed to be an epidemic of trivia, referring patients to hospital, filling in forms for state benefits. A GP interviewed in 1964 complained,

We're swamped with trivialities. This isn't the sort of work one spent years at university preparing oneself for. There's the utter futility and humiliation of a professional man who feels his training is wasted. The GP has no status because he doesn't do medicine.

(Ann Cartwright quoted in Tudor Hart, 1988, p. 85).

Such arguments revived in the mid-1990s in the 'out of hours' campaign, which again focused on the futility of trivia at another period of perceived crisis in general practice. In 1968, the Royal Commission on Medical Education found that only 23% of final-year students wanted a career in general practice, but 50% ended up there. It was thought that the general practitioner might disappear, as in the United States, where the development of specialist practices and the later development of the hospital system meant that the division between primary and secondary care was much less clear-cut (Stevens, 1966).

From the 1950s, the status of general practice rose and new concepts emerged partly from GPs themselves, but also in response to broader structural factors. General practice became an important 'front-line' service for governments increasingly concerned to contain mounting health care costs. The concept of primary health care, which had initially been a reaction to inappropriate high technology medicine in third world countries, began to be applied to developed countries as well. GPs enthusiastically embraced it.

The new vision of general practice came through 'the rehabilitation of trivia' (Jefferys and Sachs, 1983). Post-war general practice developed an extensive discourse of the normal. In 1950, the newly formed Section of General Practice of the Royal Society of Medicine held a discussion on 'What is general practice?'. The answer, it said, was 'to live amongst your patients as a definite cog in the whole machine, knowing them so well both in health and in sickness, and from birth until death' (quoted in Armstrong, 1983, p. 80). The GP's role as friend, guide and counsellor was stressed. The historical role of the GP was constructed to promote a vision of a distant era in which deep insight into family life and character was the essence of practice; this was the idea of the 'family doctor'. The work of Balint and his book, *The Doctor, his Patient and the Illness* (1956), provided GPs with a holistic model of medical practice which refuted the mind/body dichotomy of much medical practice. In theory, doctors became the ally of their patients; in practice, as Tudor Hart has argued, the Balint style was doctor centred and ignored social context. Tudor Hart himself was associated with an alternative, population-focused, research-based model of general practice which also emerged in the 1960s.

But the Balint approach was an important 'manifesto' for the group of GPs important in establishing the new College of General Practitioners in 1952. This became a powerful medico-political body and gained its royal charter in 1972. Government policy swung towards general practice and strategies to revive it. The main instrument was the Family Doctors' Charter of 1966, agreed in 1965 by the government and the General Medical Services Council of the BMA, representing GPs. Doctors were to work in common premises and to employ staff. The old post-war idea of the health centre was reactivated, this time crucially with GP support. Training was emphasised, with regular training posts in general practice and a qualifying examination. These proposals were supported by the Royal Commission on Medical Education in 1968; entry to general practice would be like entry to any other medical specialty. The (primarily) male GP was joined by middle stratum occupational groups – nurses, health visitors, social workers, receptionists – which had a predominantly female image. Attachment of workers was encouraged. In the late 1950s and early 1960s, there had been less than twenty 'attached' midwives, health visitors and nurses in the whole country. By the beginning of 1969, 25% of district nurses, 29% of health visitors and 15% of midwives employed by the local authority were working in attachment schemes. The GP 'health care team' was an invention of this period. Doctors became 'king pins in a hierarchy of dependent occupations' (Jefferys and Sachs, 1983, p. 326). The non-specialist role of the GP was reconstructed as a medical specialism. The boundaries between hospital and general practice changed as GPs reclaimed some aspects of medical work from hospitals, in particular those which related to community care. Lewis' (1997) research on the changing nature of the GP contract sees the 1960s' negotiations as deferring to the professionalism of GPs and avoiding issues of the nature and content of general practice. Such issues only came to the forefront in the 1990s.

## The decline of the Medical Officer of Health

The Medical Officer of Health could have been the unifying force in the tripartite structure of health services. But in the post-war period, the public health empire in local government began to disintegrate particularly with nationalisation of local authority hospital 'empires' over which the Medical Officer of Health had presided. Public health doctors were left with substantially reduced responsibility for a range of services: they bore some responsibility for this outcome, having previously been happy to extend their activities in whatever direction was offered, without developing a distinct vision of what 'public health' was really about (Lewis, 1986).

Relationships with GPs caused additional tensions as the latter extended their role. Health visitors, a crucial link between general practice and public health, were increasingly attached to general practices rather than their former MoH local authority 'team'. Health centres revived in the 1960s, not as local authority facilities exercising a coordinating role, but as group general practices with attached health workers. Much clinic work also passed from local authorities into general practice.

Moreover, the position of the MoH in the local authority became increasingly uncertain as ancillary health occupations defined their own professional competencies. Sanitary inspectors, who claimed autonomy in the 1950s, were renamed public health inspectors in 1956. In 1968, the Seebohm Committee recommended the removal of social workers from local authority public health to separate social work departments, in part to remove social work pressures from GPs. The differing approach of public health doctors and social workers to the concept of the 'problem family' epitomised the divergence between the two occupations, with local authorities using home helps and health visitors to inculcate domestic hygiene, while social work adopted a casework approach. The 'problem family' became part of the struggle for control between the two professional groups (Welshman, 1996).

Both Seebohm and the Todd Commission on Medical Education in 1968 promoted the 'new vision' of public health as 'community medicine'. Richard Titmuss at LSE and J. N. Morris at the London School of Hygiene and Tropical Medicine (LSHTM) envisaged a new role for public health practice which capitalised on the MoH's expertise in epidemiology, transforming him into a specialist whose knowledge and techniques would be available to colleagues in all branches of medicine. The Todd Report called community medicine the speciality practised by epidemiologists and administrators of medical services. Morris described the community physician as responsible for community diagnosis, the analysis of the health problems of the population, and therefore for providing the intelligence necessary for the efficient and effective administration of health services. Public health doctors found the idea of specialist status attractive, and the Faculty of Community Medicine was established in 1972. But they also recognised the loss of responsibility to an elected body and of the personal relationship with a community. The concept of their role shifted uneasily between the analysis of health problems and the administration of health services. How this would work in the reformed structure was unclear at the beginning of the 1970s.

*Changes in nursing*

The traditional division in British medicine had been between consultants and general practitioners (Honigsbaum, 1979), and the original arrangements for the NHS had been made without reference to nursing. Initially, the NHS was composed of three occupational hierarchies; medical, nursing and administrative. Nursing served medicine while administration facilitated the services of both doctors and nurses (Stacey, 1988). Gradually, the relationships between these different functions within the service and the balance of power altered, although much of this was not fully apparent until the late 1980s.

Nursing was propelled into the front line by the twin pressures of industrial mobilisation and cost containment (Dingwall, Rafferty and Webster, 1988, pp. 115–16). Nursing salary budgets were an obvious target for cost control; and nurse militancy grew under both Labour and Conservative governments in the 1960s. This was accompanied by changes in the character of the traditionally elitist Royal College of Nursing (RCN). In 1960, prompted by the 1957 Nurses Act which abolished the supplementary registers and substituted a single register divided into parts, the RCN removed many of its restrictions on membership. This opened the way for the College to recruit more men and to organise in the traditionally more militant (and male) area of mental nursing. A gender shift began in the balance of power within the profession. Relationships with doctors also had this dimension; nowhere more apparent than in the move, already detected before the war, to hospital-based childbirth, which reduced the power of midwives and gave it to (largely) male doctors. Chronic shortages of nurses led Ministers of Health, Powell most notably, to seek solutions through immigration from the New Commonwealth, judged at the time to be a temporary solution.

Increasingly, organisational solutions were sought for problems of health service costs. The Salmon Report of 1966 began this process for nursing. This was the 'logical corollary' (Dingwall *et al.*, p. 115) of the Ministry of Health's ambitious plans to modernise the District General Hospitals and also to achieve more efficient use of nursing labour. It led to a managerial nursing structure, developing a series of managerial grades above the ward sister and replacing the traditional hospital matron. The work structure of local authority nurses was reorganised along similar lines following the Mayston Committee Report (1969). For the first time, nurses had a management system which potentially gave them parity with other interests in the NHS. But the changes were also criticised for obstructing the development of clinical aspects of the structure. The role of the ward sister, crucial in the management of patient care, was inhibited through the implementation of the Salmon recommendations. Career progression meant leaving the bedside, and nurse leaders were divided from the bulk of the rank and file.

These changes were accompanied by the development of 'functional management' in the 1960s. Traditionally, and in the early years of the NHS, the hospital matron was in charge of the nursing service overall. The ward sister was responsible for everything which happened on her ward, from medication to the cleanliness of the ward. 'Functional management' changed this approach. Domestic supervisors became responsible for cleaning, laundry was organised on an area basis. Nurses became conscious that they should not undertake 'non-nursing' duties (Stacey, 1988, p.180).

At the same time, the role of nursing changed from another direction through the unplanned growth of what was called the 'third portal', the nursing auxiliary. This was the route by which the 'handywoman class', with its roots in nursing history, continued to provide much of the direct care of patients, especially of the chronic sick. In the 1950s there were more untrained staff working in hospitals than there had been before the war. The hostility of registered nurses to the use of such auxiliaries remained an important theme in the post-war period. The RCN remained committed to an elitist view of nurse education, and the 1964 Platt Committee on the subject saw only educational solutions to organisational problems. Dingwall *et al.* contrast this report, which stressed the benefits for individual nurses, with the Royal Commission on Medical Education which was more attuned to the need to adapt medical education to the changing pattern of health care needs and services. The Briggs Committee, originating just before the 1970 general election, was initially a strategy by the Labour government to deflect short-term political problems, in this case militancy and discontent among nurses. Its report (1972), which led to legislation at the end of the 1970s (see below), paid attention to structural detail rather than to the nature of nursing work (Dingwall *et al.*, 1988, pp. 206 ff).

## The growth in health care occupations

In general, the numbers and types of non-medical workers in health related occupations expanded in the post-war years. The British Medical Association (BMA) lobbied the government for statutory powers over allied professionals under the NHS. Ministry of Health policy was to reject direct BMA control over para-medical occupations. This was not, as Larkin has argued, in itself a rejection of medical dominance (Larkin, 1993, p.1341). A more effective type of medical control was to be linked to overall state supervision. This objective lay behind the Cope proposals (1951), the first of a number of post-war attempts to address concerns about the fragmentation of medicine. Cope's recommendations for a body to oversee the training and practice of all medical auxiliaries foundered on para-medical opposition to medical dominance. These professionals wanted 'an occupational "commonwealth" rather than an imperial mode of hierarchical relationships' (p. 1342), collaborative relationships rather than a rigid professional hierarchy with medicine at the summit. By 1960, all the main para-medical professions had achieved state registration, the opticians through the 1958 Opticians' Act, and the rest through the 1960 Professions Supplementary to Medicine Act. A final supervisory council, despite medical opposition, balanced doctors and auxiliaries in equal numbers. The Act, as Larkin points out, was a compromise, with the state as umpire. It was a matter of redrawing the boundaries without equalising all the parties. The expansion of hospital-based medicine also led to a growth in hospital-based scientific and technical services in an unplanned and uncoordinated way. Despite the report of the Zuckerman Committee in 1968, efforts of such workers to improve their status made little progress in this period (Webster, 1996).

## From environmentalism to personal prevention

Public health as an occupational category, as we have seen in the third section (pp. 44–5), was redefining itself as 'community medicine', although it was in fact becoming more remote from 'the community' and more closely identified with hospital-based medicine. Public health issues also underwent change in this period. The shift can be broadly characterised as a move away from environmentalism towards a greater degree of individual responsibility for the maintenance of health. This emphasis on the 'personal' informed a number of developments in health policy. It was accompanied, in particular in the 1960s, by the 'deregulation of personal life' in significant areas and the replacement of areas of legal regulation by medical surveillance and control.

### *Traditional public health: vaccination, environmentalism*

The immediate post-war period was, however, marked by the utilisation of the traditional, if not uncontroversial, public health strategy of vaccination against infectious disease. BCG vaccination against tuberculosis was gradually adopted in Britain during the 1950s. Some commentators criticised Britain for being behind other countries in adopting this approach. The introduction of vaccination in the 1950s was slower than in the Scandinavian countries because of the British investment in hospital beds for the treatment of TB. The curative not the preventive model was dominant. (Bryder, 1999). But TB was giving place to polio as a major epidemic disease. Polio outbreaks occurred in Britain in 1947, 1950 and 1957. Webster (1996) has detailed the history of British attempts at various strategies of vaccination between 1955 and 1960 (pp. 129–31). In a story which has some parallels with the introduction of testing for HIV some thirty years later, British authorities initially rejected use of the US Salk vaccine and favoured development of a British vaccine, which, it was reckoned, would have a greater degree of safety. An American vaccine would also have increased the level of dollar imports. Failures in supply led eventually to successive importations of the Salk vaccine together with gradually widening campaigns of vaccination. A recrudescence of the disease in the early 1960s eventually, after initial delay, brought widespread use of the Sabin vaccine, a live attenuated vaccine, administered orally. Gould (1995) gives a personal insight into the meaning of polio for a sufferer.

In the 1950s, public health still had environmental focus. The question of air pollution underlined this environmentalism (Parker, 1986). The 'great London smog' of 1952 which lasted five days and killed 4,000 people, brought matters to a head. The Clean Air Act of 1956 established smokeless zones and controlled domestic smoke emissions for the first time. Its passing was the result of pressure from the National Society for Smoke Abatement, which was a cross-party group of MPs and a few MoHs. It was a notable success. Two million tons of smoke were discharged into the atmosphere in 1954; by 1979, this had fallen to 700,000 tons, a reduction of 65%. The public health profession had little formal involvement in the campaign. The clean air campaign was in that sense transitional towards the newer style 'single issue' campaigns of the 1960s and after. These operated in some respects like the nineteenth-century pressure group campaigns round anti-vaccination or the Contagious Diseases Acts. Increasingly, public health action and the 'new public health' was expressed through that type of activity rather than through the public health profession. These changes will be discussed below (chapter 4).

*The rise of personal and health education*

The very success of the environmental campaign encouraged the belief that such environmental problems had been disposed of. Further campaigns aiming at environmental change, for example, the fluoridation of water, had little success. The focus of public health began to turn towards health issues in the context of individual responsibility. The background to this was the changing balance between infectious and chronic disease, which has already been mentioned. Health education rather than treatment became a major focus of policy. The rise of smoking as a public health issue epitomised this change. The publication in 1962 of the first Royal College of Physicians (RCP) report on *Smoking and Health* was a significant watershed. The original RCP Committee had intended to look at environmental as well as individual matters, but the smoking issue was given precedence. The committee's report brought into the public policy domain the epidemiological researches of Richard Doll and Sir Austin Bradford Hill at the London School of Hygiene and Tropical Medicine (LSHTM) in the 1940s and 50s, on the relationship between smoking and lung cancer. This conjuncture of events encapsulated a number of significant developments in science and in policy. For science, it endorsed the role of epidemiology and a change of scientific 'gaze' from direct biomedically influenced causation to statistical inference. For policy, it helped initiate a post-war health policy based round the notion of individual responsibility and personal avoidance of risk, a policy which skilfully combined elements of morality with the concepts of science (Berridge, 1998).

The rise of these preventive approaches was inextricably bound up with health education as a major public health strategy. The war had seen a greater focus on health education, as for example in the war time campaigns on VD. These wartime appeals in army health education to enlightened self-interest were a foretaste of later emphases in post-war health education, replacing the moral element common in the First World War. The Central Council for Health Education, already mentioned in chapter 2, was supported by the Treasury in its work during the war, taking responsibility for sex education (education on VD) from the British Social Hygiene Council. But after the war, little was done. Funding of the Central

Council moved to the local authorities, and the Ministry of Health contribution ended in the 1950s. The Treasury was anxious at this stage not to resume responsibility for health education. MoHs saw possibilities in health education after the demise of their hospital role. Health education officers began to be appointed by the local authorities and school health education became more of a priority.

The Cohen Committee on Health Education, 1959–64, argued that health education was needed over a greater range of subjects and that popular journalism and mass marketing techniques were important. The Cohen Report also recommended a strong central health education board to replace the CCHE. In 1968, the Health Education Council (HEC), funded by the DHSS, replaced the Central Council. The new Council was to occupy an ambiguous role between central government and the periphery. But its establishment symbolised a much greater commitment in government policy making to questions of prevention, with pressure coming both from the English CMO, Sir George Godber, and from the Scottish Office, which set up its own separate departmental Health Education Unit (Webster, 1996, pp. 135–8). The new HEC had an uncertain start with changes of Director and other leadership. But it symbolised a new and more direct emphasis on health education as a strategy and a focus on personal habits which was to be taken further in policy documents of the late 70s (see below, chapter 4, fourth section, pp. 87–8).

The Cohen Committee and the RCP smoking report both laid stress on the role of the media. Increasingly, the techniques of mass advertising were brought into the health field, in particular in the 1970s. Doctors became more conscious of the media and television in particular as a means of conveying the medical ethos. Karpf sees the television series, *Your Life in Their Hands* (*YLITH*), first transmitted in 1958, as a watershed, shifting media attention from the self-reliant collectivism of the wartime years to a concern for 'high tech' medicine and for 'medical cure' (Karpf, 1988). The 1960s and to a greater extent the 1970s also saw the media being used by doctors to convey the new emphasis on healthy living and lifestyles. The 1962 Royal College of Physicians report on smoking took great care over its presentation in the media, with press conferences, a cheap edition and brief summaries of the material. Charles Fletcher, presenter of *YLITH* and drafter of the RCP report was a key person in these medical media developments. These brought into the public domain the new emphasis within medicine on the techniques of epidemiology and of the social survey.

## *The deregulation of personal life*

The 'mediatisation' of medicine gave publicity in the 1960s to changes which Lewis has characterised as the 'deregulation of personal life' (Lewis, 1992a). The advent of the contraceptive pill, abortion (1967), easier divorce (from 1969) and a more relaxed attitude to homosexuality all characterised a more 'permissive' era. Family planning services became more easily available. The contraceptive pill was a woman-controlled method of contraception – but also the first mass medication of healthy women. As such it began a pharmaceutical trend carried forward through hormone replacement therapy and other 'preventive medication' such as tamoxifen for those at risk of breast cancer (Leathard, 1980). After the war, the baby boom and the reassertion of the importance of women's role as wife and mother in the home had led to contraceptive services once more being given a back seat. Riley has argued that the closure of nurseries after the war owed more to interdepartmental tensions in Whitehall and a desire to transfer costs to the local authorities (as was the case with health education) rather than to the maternal deprivation theories of John Bowlby and others (Riley, 1981). But these views were common among psychologists even before the war, and were accepted by women themselves. The lack of interest in family planning provision initially owed more to fears of a return to the low birth rates of the 1930s. For family planning, a key development was the advent of the contraceptive pill, approved by the Medical Advisory Panel of the Family Planning Association in 1961. By 1964, there were about 480,000 women on the pill in Britain. The Church of England gave its approval to contraception. Official support for the provision of birth control came at the end of the 1960s, when legislation in 1967 enabled local health authorities to provide services on a general basis. Passed with little controversy because of the furore over the parallel Abortion Bill, the law in fact made little difference, and services continued often to be provided by a voluntary organisation, the Family Planning Association, acting on behalf of these authorities. Debate over the provision of free family planning services continued into the first half of the 1970s, stimulated by what Webster (1996, p. 414) calls an 'ill-sorted alliance of demographers, racists, social liberals and feminists'. Concern about high immigrant birth rates and the reproduction of the 'unfit' added to the pressure on the government. The issue was in part resolved, although not to the liking of some of the campaigners, when GPs were given responsibility for family planning in 1975 and a prescription charge was imposed. The desire of GPs to keep control of, and fees from, prescribing the pill, added to resistance to easier availability. In the late 1960s and early 70s, too, there was rising concern about the safety of the contraceptive pill, and in particular its possible association with thrombosis. Marks (1999) shows how these drug safety issues were identified and acted on earlier in Britain than in the US. This differing cross national experience she ascribes to different national cultures of research, different health care systems, modes of drug regulation and consumer cultures.

In other areas, 'deregulation' or rather the establishment of different forms of regulation proceeded apace. The Sexual Offences Act of 1967 carried out in part the proposals of the earlier Wolfenden Report by decriminalising adult male homosexual activities. The notion of homosexuality as a medical condition was still seen as a more liberal alternative in the 1960s. The 1967 Abortion Act introduced the possibility of 'social' as well as medical reasons for lawful termination of pregnancy (Brookes, 1988). Public outrage had been stimulated by the thalidomide disaster in the late 1950s and early 1960s and at the lengths women had to go to obtain an abortion. The Abortion Law Reform Association, which played a key role, had been active since the 1930s. But the clash between those who wished to curtail the 1967 Act and those who wanted abortion on demand continued. Even the 1974 report of a committee to review the Act under Justice Lane, which gave it broad support, did little to quieten debate. Weeks (1981) comments that these reforms were ultimately very limited. They were also marked by a tendency for notions of sickness to fill the gap vacated by the idea of moral failure; 'while the law took one step back, the medical profession took one forward' (Weeks, 1981, p. 267). Doctors played a key role both in access to safe abortion and to the new 'scientific' contraceptive pill, which was available only on prescription. Deviant behaviour was medicalised and the rules were operated by medical professionals. A rise in illegitimate births and in divorce marked the 1960s (tables in Lewis, 1992b, p. 45). Despite criticism by some historians of these changes, they represented undoubted advances, and certainly a more open climate operated than before.

# 4
# Health policy, health and society, 1974–1990s

The quadrupling of oil prices by the producers in 1973 plunged the Western economies into crisis, a crisis which affected the welfare state and its funding above all. The post-war consensus round welfare policy was disrupted, and a new Right wing orthodoxy on welfare emerged in the 1970s, finding its political expression in the Thatcher and Major governments of the 1980s and 90s. Much of this panic about public spending was expressed through health and welfare issues, which became increasingly contentious from the mid-1970s. The British health experience is the focus of this book, but to some extent the country was experiencing perceived problems which affected health care systems around the world. Industrialised countries rationalised their fears about public spending through delineation of 'health problems' which came to define the policy agendas. The burden of chronic illness, the rise of new infectious diseases, the growing numbers of elderly; questions of the organisation and funding of services, such as the need to control costs, improve accountability and efficiency, monitor effectiveness and establish priorities – in some form, these issues affected most countries. The role of medicine and unquestioned professional dominance in the health arena was under strain. Ever-increasing costs and uncertainties about the relationship between medical care, formal health services and health status brought a more questioning attitude both to the role of medicine and to the relationship between medicine and the role of the state. Health *outputs* as well as *inputs* came on to the policy agenda for the first time.

As Webster argues (1993, p.128, and 1996), in terms of practical policy if not political rhetoric, the parties were closer together than sometimes appeared. Governments of the Right, while introducing significant change in health services, did not carry out the scale of change which some influential thinkers would have wished. Such changes have taken place against the background of the increased burden of chronic disease. With the arrival of legionella, salmonella and, most urgently, AIDS in the 1980s, the balance between chronic and infectious disease did appear to be shifting back towards the infections.

## *Critiques of health and medicine*

The theoretical attack on the power of medicine at the beginning of this period came from a number of different directions. The philosopher and theologian Ivan Illich, for example, argued in the 1970s that beside the beneficial effects of medicine had also to be set iatrogenesis, or, the harmful effects of medical practice. For Illich, surgery and drug treatment were new forms of epidemic. Other critics argued that medicine exercised socio-political strategies of power and control in the name of apparently objective and value-free scientific knowledge. The French philosopher-historian Michel Foucault emphasised the 'great confinement' of the asylum under medical surveillance influencing historical work on insanity and hence the post-war drive for deinstitutionalisation in mental health. His analysis of the 'medical gaze' also underpinned innovative historical sociology which analysed post-war epidemiology, general practice and paediatric medicine in terms of its function as surveillance (Armstrong, 1983). Such analyses were part of an emergent radical critique of the power of medicine, allied to the developing feminist analysis of the gender dimension of health care issues, also with a strong historical component (Finch and Groves, 1983). The feminist analysis is discussed below. The ethicist Ian Kennedy caused a furore in his Reith lectures, later published as *The Unmasking of Medicine* (Kennedy, 1981).

Perhaps the most influential argument in terms of medicine and of policy was that advanced by Thomas McKeown, Professor of Social Medicine at Birmingham University. The 'McKeown thesis' was that much of the major burden of infectious and other disease in the nineteenth century had begun to decline well before medical 'magic bullets' were available to deal with it. More important, in

McKeown's view, were general changes in living standards, and in particular in standards of nutrition towards the end of the century. McKeown's historical perspective focused on the eighteenth to twentieth centuries. But his arguments had considerable impact in health planning at both national and international levels in the 1970s and 80s. They justified the shift towards primary care and prevention and away from 'high tech' hospital-based medicine which will be discussed below (McKeown, 1976). The growing economic critique of medicine was also increasingly powerful from the 1970s. Cochrane, for example, in his *Effectiveness and Efficiency*, identified areas which needed evaluation such as the use of therapies, of health care settings and lengths of stay in treatment facilities (Cochrane, 1972). The numbers of health economists working for health services grew rapidly in this period.[1]

In the 1980s and 90s, such arguments were appropriated by the 'Radical Right' to justify policies of cost containment, of restriction of medical autonomy and a focus on lower cost forms of health provision. As Lewis comments, 'The rhetoric of prevention has . . . been harnessed to the cause of cost control' (Lewis, 1992a, p. 342). The 1970s demands for increased patient power and incipient consumerism were also redefined in a new political context as the patient's rights as a consumer of health services. But consumer rights were essentially defined in a negative sense, through reduction of the power of some health care providers rather than through a positive desire to involve such 'consumers' in the running of health services and the definition of patterns of provision. This was not a democratic or collectivist vision of popular participation.

## The organisation of services

The 1974 reorganisation of the NHS came out of a period which Klein (1995) has characterised as one of the 'politics of technocratic change'. Issues of costs and access were again dealt with through organisational change. The detail of reorganisation and its failure to achieve its objectives have already been discussed in chapter 3. The

[1] J. Hutton, 'The costs of health care; an historical and economic perspective', unpublished paper, 1995.

service was more complex than that established in 1948 and only slightly more unified. Somewhat different arrangements were made for Wales, Scotland and Northern Ireland, which, until reorganisation, had had similar structures to those in England. The main difference was in Scotland where there was no regional tier of administration and the Scottish Office dealt directly with fifteen health boards, divided into districts (Ham, 1992, p. 29). These direct links may have intensified the ability of Scotland to develop distinctly different patterns of service provision and health initiatives, a tendency which was apparent for example in the health education area.

The 1974 reorganisation satisfied no one, and its deficiencies were recognised by the 1979 Report of the Royal Commission on the NHS. Its report provided 'an overwhelming – though not uncritical – endorsement of the NHS's achievements' (Klein, 1995, p. 133). The following consultative document, *Patients First,* issued under the incoming Conservative government, introduced a focus on the patient (borrowed from the radical critique of medicine), which informed government rhetoric into the 1990s. In practice, however, a solution was again sought in reorganisation. A further one in 1982 abolished the area tier of administration and established 192 District Health Authorities. The District was to be the new focus, both providing and planning services. Changes following the NHS management inquiry (1983) by Sir Roy Griffiths increased the role of professional management. General managers, the solution which Sir Keith Joseph had been unable to carry forward at the time of the earlier reorganisation, were appointed at regional, district and hospital unit level, in place of the consensus management teams which had operated since 1974.

General practitioner organisation again remained independent and outside this framework. General practice also remained largely outside the financial constraints which began to affect the hospital service in the late 1970s. Hospitals had always been a major consumer of NHS resources, around 70% in the 1970s (Webster, 1996, p. 808). The introduction in 1976–7 of cash limits for health authority budgets meant that authorities were no longer automatically compensated for inflation. The responsibility for making choices about spending decisions had been pushed to the local level and 'cuts' could therefore be blamed on districts and not central government. The impact of this change was greatest in London, primarily because of the parallel adoption of the RAWP formula recommended by the Resource Allocation Working Party in 1976, a new formula for allocating NHS resources between the regions. Its principal innovation, which was to become increasingly important in the 1990s, was the inclusion of measures of need among the factors used to determine the allocation of funds. The operation of RAWP did manage to achieve a measure of redistribution between the regions. Cash limits applied to the hospital sector and not to primary health care, which greatly benefited GPs (see Webster, 1996, p. 133 and table).

Le Grand, Winter and Woolley (1991) stress continuities throughout the 1970s and the first half of the 80s. The major concerns of governments were the same; managerial reorganisation, regional and other inequalities and the Cinderella services. For the latter, both governments made commitments to spending on priority groups – the elderly, mentally ill and mentally handicapped – and to developing community care. The Labour government's 1976 consultative document, *Priorities for Health and Personal Social Services in England*, was the first to recognise the need to set priorities in health care. The Labour government increased spending on hospital-based inpatient and outpatient services and increased the volume of spending on each elderly person. The Conservatives spent less on hospital services for the elderly and cut back those for the mentally handicapped, but spending on health visiting and district nursing increased substantially (Le Grand, Winter and Woolley, 1991, p.115).

However, it was the ideological differences of this period which dominated public attention. Perhaps the chief of these was over the removal of pay beds from NHS hospitals, an overriding concern of Barbara Castle as Secretary of State in 1974–6; Webster (1996, p. 627) judges this policy to have been a failure, succeeding ultimately in stimulating rather than repressing the private sector of health care. There were also debates over the contracting out of services; and tax concessions to private medicine. In the early 1980s, the effect of these changes was dramatic with rapid increases in the number of subscribers to private medicine. There was a 26% increase in the number of subscribers to private medical insurance in 1980, followed by a 13% increase in 1981 (Le Grand, Winter and

Woolley, 1991, p. 93). However, this rate of increase subsequently fell (table 4). Use of private beds in NHS hospitals continued to fall, and the private sector outside the NHS remained small, although making a significant contribution in the area of elective surgery. In the 1990s, however, there were signs that, in London at least, the role of private medicine within NHS Hospital Trusts was becoming increasingly important.[2]

## *Technology, rationing and the evaluation of health care*

The rapid technological developments in medicine in the immediate post-war period described in chapter 3 continued and intensified in pace in this period. Webster (1996, pp. 754–6) and Rivett (1998) provide a guide to the major events. A variety of advanced technologies were brought together in intensive care units and special care baby units. Replacement and transplantation surgery became routine. Such innovation was among the factors contributing to the rising demand for health care. Rationing had always been practised within the NHS through the activities of consultants (Stanton, 1999). But in the 1980s, issues of funding, rationing and access to services came to figure high on the policy agenda, and became overt rather than covert. The pursuit of cost-effectiveness brought with it a variety of different mechanisms for controlling costs and for trying to achieve equity and effectiveness. These included techniques such as the quality-adjusted life year (QALY); medical audit; and the randomised controlled trial (RCT), which became a kind of 'gold standard' of evaluation. There was much interest in the Oregon experiment in the United States, where, in the late 1980s, health planners used public opinion surveys to decide how to ration treatments. Studies by health economists expanded after the mid-1970s. The work of the American health economist, Alain Enthoven, who argued that quality and economy could go hand in hand, hugely influenced government thinking in the second half of the 1980s.

These developments also had their impact in the area of drug therapy. Drug treatments had further expanded from the 1970s

[2] *Guardian*, 25 March 1996 (p. 69).

with the advent of, among others, beta-blockers for the relief of angina and hypertension, new anaesthetics and a greater range of anticoagulants (Webster, 1996, p. 755). The Labour government had initially aimed in 1974 to seek some form of nationalisation of the pharmaceutical industry, but all governments of this period in fact took a more relaxed attitude to the industry, liberalising the rules governing the introduction of new drugs (Abraham, 1995). A 'limited list' of drugs in November 1984 established restrictions on the GPs' right to prescribe and attempted to control NHS drug budgets. By the end of the 1980s, the process of drug regulation had moved further in the industry's favour. Following the Evans/Cunliffe Report in 1989, the Medicines Division of the DH became the Medicines Control Agency, almost entirely funded as a commercial operation, by industry fees. Abraham (1995) sees a move towards a greater degree of industry self-regulation.

## The further reorganisation of the NHS

Allsop has identified a series of criticisms of the NHS which emerged by the mid-1980s. These included uncertain costs because of professional autonomy; central negotiation with powerful professional groups; lack of information about costs and clinical effectiveness; uncertainty about outcomes; rising demand; central resourcing and capital starvation (Allsop, 1995b, p. 111). The government set up a review of the NHS as a whole at the end of the 1980s. The review took longer than expected, perhaps delayed by the splitting of the DHSS into component parts and the appointment of a new Secretary of State for Health, Kenneth Clarke. A White Paper, *Working for Patients*, appeared in January 1989; this was implemented in April 1991. Klein (1995, p. 176) has considered a number of explanations of how this came about. These include the perennial problem of financing ever-increasing demands for health care; a government in its third term at last able to forge ahead with its own agenda; the widening of the horizons of the possible after reform in other areas. To these were added the fact that the government was able to draw on a wide variety of ideas offering a rich policy menu; and the NHS was following a pattern of reorganisation common, through information technology, to large organisations everywhere. Webster has argued in addition and plausibly that 'rising public expectations' of health care also encompassed a desire to hold on to existing services and not see them eroded. The debates, at least from the public perspective, were not just about quality issues but about access to treatments and procedures which were potentially life saving (Webster, 1993, p. 134). Mohan (1995) sees the reforms as driven by political dogma, while Le Grand and Glennerster see the changes as responses both to consumer demand and scarce resources.

The central paradox of the NHS Review was that no proposals for changing the method of funding emerged despite the perception of financial crisis. The NHS remained a universal, tax-financed health care system. The government once again sought refuge in organisational solutions. This time it was the radical creation of an internal market in health care. The main proposals were for hospitals to 'opt out' of local health authority control and become self- governing NHS Trusts; for district health authorities to contract with the newly independent hospitals to provide services and with community services, also transformed into trusts, and with other providers as well; for large GP practices to be given budgets of their own with which they could purchase outside services and treatment for their patients. There was an extension of medical audit, and changes in the composition of health authorities to make them more managerial, in particular through the removal of local authority and trade union representatives.

The government therefore committed itself to the notion of quasi-markets, an idea marketed by LSE-based health economists rather than the University of York 'firm' who had dominated the health economics scene throughout the 1980s. As Klein points out, this was a 'mimic market', where financial incentives would be used not to generate profits, as in the market place, but to sharpen the incentives of everyone working in the NHS to make more efficient use of public funds (Klein, 1995, p. 184). The improvement of the NHS was tied to an organisational solution which offered the prospect of reduced public expenditure. Responsibility for spending decisions was once again devolved to the local level. DHAs were given budgets according to the size and demographic composition of their populations. By assessing the needs of local populations via research ('needs assessment') and by other means, they could in theory obtain the most appropriate packages of services from providers. The key principle was that of 'money follows patients'. The overall idea was that the internal market would allow the most productive units to prosper and the least effective to wither away.

The 1948 settlement had aimed at the integration of services. Health authorities had been planners, owners, employers and providers of services in their area. This was replaced by the principle of separation of functions and a contractual relationship between purchaser and provider. The post-1948 model of health care, what Klein calls 'health care as Church', was in part replaced by the market-oriented 'health care as garage' model (Klein, 1995, p. 248). The role of the state was changing. Lewis sees these developments as establishing central control of finance with the devolving of responsibility to the local level. The reforms were clearly influenced by parallel developments in educational policy and changes in local government service provision, where the contractual relationship was also used to inject an element of competition into services. Central government financial control was increased while local authorities bore the responsibility for managing the changes.

Allsop (1995b, pp. 115–16) identifies a number of criticisms of the changes. Some argued that competition was inappropriate for health care; others that there was no true market in health care. There was uncertainty and lack of accountability in the new arrangements, arising from the lack of formal mechanisms for local control of spending decisions. The 'reforms' were introduced with speed; and the issue of funding was not addressed. In fact, contracting itself brought extra costs. The fragmentation of the service made it more difficult than ever to plan and to ensure equity in distribution and access to services. The 1990s reorganisation adopted solutions which had been considered, and then rejected by the Conservative government of the early 1970s. The NHS gained a Chief Executive and was placed under the NHS Management Executive (NHSME), the separate corporation which had also been considered in the 1970s. The 1994 Banks Report which divided up NHSME responsibilities with the Department of Health, gave the Executive responsibility for both policy formulation and implementation, leaving the DH with a mixture of other responsibilities. This, so it was argued, marked the victory of the NHS over the civil service (Klein, 1995, p. 215; Florin, 1999). The removal in 1996 of the regional tier of health authorities and their transmutation into eight regional offices of the Executive further strengthened the power of the centre. Klein sees this development as a greater degree of centralisation rather than decentralisation. In his view, the NHS, half a century after its inception, at last became a national service, with lines of accountability running firmly to the centre. Authority chairmen and non-executives owed their positions to ministerial favour rather than, as before, to local power bases. The NHS's dependence on central public funds also inevitably centralised and politicised accountability, as it had done since its inception. Other commentators, for example Mohan (1995), see more of a tension between local autonomy and central control.

The reforms carried forward the managerial tendencies apparent in organisational changes since the 1970s. Improving management within the NHS had been a concern for organisations such as the King's Fund since the 1960s, but it was in the 1970s that these developments gathered pace. The introduction of general management in the 1980s had seemed to take these developments a stage further and allow real power and control over doctors, at least according to the general managers interviewed by Strong and Robinson (1990). But how far power had shifted from medicine to managers in the post-1991 NHS remained a matter of debate. The clinical autonomy of individual consultants had certainly been reduced and managers were able, in theory at least, to call doctors to account. How this worked in practice varied considerably according to local conditions. Treatment decisions, and consequent expenditure, as Harrison and Wistow note (1993, p. 19), were still primarily controlled by doctors. 'Clinical directorates', headed by consultants, were an increasingly common tier of management at the level of the medical specialty. Doctors themselves 'went managerial'. A further significant development was the development of 'collective professional autonomy'. Doctors, through their national professional organisations, took greater responsibility for regulating their own standards, with intensive production of protocols and guidelines laying down standards for good practice (Klein, 1995, p. 243). The case of medical audit, where doctors were successful in retaining control of the process and in preventing it from becoming a management tool, illustrates this point. Doctors incorporated and controlled management tools. At the level of central advice giving, too, doctors had retained their place as expert advisers to the Department and as members of the central advisory committees which expanded in various health policy areas (alcohol and illicit drugs were two examples) in the 1970s after changes in the formal health service advisory machinery (Webster, 1996). But in the 1980s and 90s, these also underwent change with a greater input of non-medical advisory personnel (Berridge, 1997).

How far competition exists also remained debatable. In most areas, there was no real competition among providers. In practice, market forces were regulated and no Trusts allowed to fail. Increments for teaching and research were funded from the centre; and measures were introduced to protect particular hospitals. The internal market created particular difficulties for higher-cost teaching hospitals. In London, proposals from the King's Fund and the Tomlinson Report in 1992 suggested wholesale closure of hospital facilities in central London and their substitution by improved primary care facilities. There were managed closures. But when University College Hospital was threatened with closure through the removal of contracts to a lower cost source of supply in 1993, Virginia Bottomley, as Secretary of State for Health, intervened and the HAs were required to keep their contracts with the hospital (Allsop, 1995a, p. 183). In other ways, too, markets did not operate. Money did follow patients, but the amount was not elastic and efficiency was not always rewarded by more funding.

The reduction in the power of professionals was to be achieved by opposing a consumer-led range of services to a professionally-led care delivery system (Lewis, 1992a, p. 344). But the effect of the reforms on the 'patient as consumer' remained equivocal. The Patients' Charter (1991) gave patients what Allsop calls 'a confusing mixture of citizens' rights and customer service standards' (Allsop, 1995a, p. 191). Consumerism replaced citizenship, with all the loss of rights that entailed; ultimately a diffusion of responsibility resulted. Patients complained more throughout the 1980s and after the reforms, and services became more consumer sensitive. But participation, as for example, in needs assessment, was limited. As Klein notes, the dynamics of the new model NHS were driven not by consumers, but by purchasers; health authorities and fundholding GPs became proxy consumers. The democratic accountability of the service was reduced and the position of CHCs weakened.

The reforms built on some long-standing tensions in the health care arena. To the historically minded, it seemed that in many respects there was a return to the pre-NHS fragmentation of services. The self-governing hospital trusts recalled memories of the pre-war voluntary hospital system. The rise of the fundholding GP and the later development of GP commissioning consortia gave general practice more of a pivotal role in the long-standing tension between GPs and consultants. Consultants became accountable to fundholding GPs, who took more interest in what consultants did because of their financial responsibility. Health authorities, too, were forced to court general practitioners, devolving authority to consortia in order to prevent 'opt out' into fundholding with its consequent effect on authority budgets and planning. The reforms intensified the moves towards primary care also inherent in other arms of government health policy and which are discussed below (fourth section, pp. 76–8).

There were unintended as well as intended consequences of the reforms. But at the time of writing (1997), any final evaluation of effects was impossible, in part because of political changes. The new Labour government intended to introduce GP-commissioning consortia. Evaluation had never been part of the original design for change. The Conservative government was convinced of the need to introduce market principles and resisted all pressure either for 'piloting' the reforms in certain areas, or for formal evaluation. Research, despite the injection of an intended link between evidence and practice through the establishment in 1991 of a centrally-led NHS Research and Development Strategy, was clearly not of importance at the macro policy level although it had more influence on micro policy issues.

## *Continuity or change?*

These events are very recent history, and have been the subject of political and policy, rather than of historical, debate. However, the historical theme of continuity and/or change has impinged on discussions. Le Grand, Winter and Woolley, in a piece which appeared in 1990, argue for continuity in policies towards the NHS up to 1988, followed by radical change, at least on the delivery side through the NHS reforms (Le Grand, Winter and Woolley, 1991). Lewis argues for continuity *and* change. Issues such as cost and patterns of organisation have a long history. She considers the willingness of the state to attack medical autonomy and to consider a reduction of its own role to be significant new departures (Lewis, 1992a, p. 345). Webster argues that in practical terms, the service user may notice little difference; 'the promised revolution may turn out to represent an unexpected degree of historical continuity' (1993, p. 136). Klein also seems to argue for a degree of continuity, although recognising that the evidence on which to make assessments is mostly lacking (Klein, 1995). Allsop's recent analysis argues for consensus over policy until the 1980s then followed by change (Allsop, 1995b). Problems which had been apparent throughout the history of the NHS remained. There were still tensions between cost containment and adequate funding; between medical and managerial models of decision making; between hospital and primary care; over forms of accountability; and between local and centralised policy making. Health care reform was one of the international epidemics of the 1990s. Britain was different from other countries, with the exception of New Zealand, in being able both to initiate and successfully to implement health care reform. The NHS had been a most efficient service taken in the context of other national health care systems. Yet it was the system which underwent most change. The crucial issue of underfunding remained unaddressed; and for a historian it was symbolic that the first Labour government budget in 1997 adopted the 2.5% growth norm which had been considered 'about right' since the earliest days of the service.

## Community care and lay care

Confusion and imprecision has surrounded the term 'community care' when a policy of care in the community has been a priority for successive governments since the end of the Second World War (Hunter, 1993 p. 122). Lewis (1997) has pointed out that community care was the focus in the 1980s, while by the 1990s, primary

care was centre stage. Neither were taken together in policy documents and what they actually meant was little discussed.

## Mental health

Despite the failure to move resources over to the local authorities,
community care policy none the less continued to be a corner-stone
of policy throughout the 1970s. The 1975 White Paper, *Better
Services for the Mentally Ill*, emphasised the need for normalisation –
enabling people with dependency needs to live a normal life. Similar
strategies underpinned policies for the disabled and mentally handicapped. The move against long stay institutions continued, fuelled by the ideological critique of institutional, and especially asylum, care. Micale and Porter (1994) point out that the history
which supported that critique owed much to physicians as well as
professional historians. Jones (1993), however, notes that the primary focus of reformers in organisations such as MIND was the
safeguarding of human rights rather than involvement in the development of community care. Larry Gostin of MIND campaigned for
the introduction of stricter criteria for compulsory committal and
the strengthening of patients' rights to resist unwanted treatments.
These efforts found their expression in the 1983 Mental Health Act,
which Unsworth sees as a 'considerable revival of legalism' (Unsworth, 1987). This emphasis on human rights transferred, in part
through the influence of Gostin and Jonathan Mann, across into
self-help movements around AIDS, as will be discussed below. The
mental health campaign was an important avenue for the introduction of an American-style emphasis on legally enforceable rights
(Gostin is an American lawyer) into the British health arena. In
America anti-psychiatry campaigners had resorted to the law but
this legalism was remote from the British tradition. The role of law
and the contract assumed increasing importance, along with the
concepts of ethics and of human rights, in British health policy in
the 1980s.

Community care policy received a further impetus at the end of
the 1970s with the election of the Thatcher government. Publicity
given to the increasing preponderance of the elderly in the population together with the incoming government's attachment to 'an

inter-connected trinity of family, private market, and voluntary sector' gave community care revived prominence. The 1981 White Paper, *Growing Older*, stressed the importance of informal care; the primary sources of support and care for elderly people were to be 'informal and voluntary'. 'Care in the community must increasingly mean care by the community'.[3] This was the initial stance taken by the new government. However, Hunter notes that under Norman Fowler, Secretary of State for Social Services from 1981 to 1987, the previous emphasis on voluntary and informal care was moderated and was replaced by a new emphasis on the shared responsibility of public agencies and informal carers (Hunter, 1993, p. 125).

Policy also had unintended consequences. Changes in the social security system in the 1980s resulted in an enormous growth of private residential homes for old people. Howard Glennerster notes that an almost perfect voucher scheme grew up by accident. 'Families could choose a home for their elderly relative and the state would pay. This maximised choice and consumer power' (Glennerster, 1995, p. 208). But the result was that public expenditure in this area rose from £10 million in 1979 to £2,072 million by 1991; there was a rise in institutionalisation in the 1980s. This unintended consequence was counter to official policy on community care, which was to keep people in their own homes for as long as possible.

A series of reports, including the influential 1986 report of the Audit Commission, considered what could be done about this perverse incentive to residential care. The solution was found by Roy Griffiths. He had already reported on management in the NHS and produced a further report on community care in 1988. The Griffiths Report was notable for its recommendation to make the local authorities responsible for community care, a strategy which, it was widely believed, would be unacceptable to the Thatcher government which had sought to remove the power of these authorities. This option was, however, acceptable to Mrs Thatcher because local social services departments became largely purchasing agencies, or 'enabling authorities'. The extra money they received was to be spent on services in the private sector, not primarily on local authority services. As Glennerster notes, there was no real private sector apart from private residential homes, so much of the

---

[3] Quoted in J. Lewis, 'Making recent community and primary care policy', lecture, LSHTM, 1997.

money found its way back to them (Glennerster, 1995 p.209). The changes were introduced by the NHS and Community Care Act of 1990. From April 1993, the social security system ceased to provide support for new residents in private and voluntary homes. Local authorities had a duty to assess the needs of anyone believed to require community care; services were to be provided either by the authority or by purchasing them from a private or voluntary agency. The authority was charged with drawing up a community care plan. The main provisions of the Act were delayed and only came into force in April 1993, with a special transitional community care grant available, of which 85% of the social security element had to be spent in the private sector.

The long-term effects of these changes remained to be seen at the time of writing. Social services departments had faced huge changes. They were uncomfortable with the notion of markets, competition and purchasing, rather than providing services (Wistow, quoted in Glennerster, 1995). Lewis' interim assessment of implementation in a number of different authorities found policy being shaped from the bottom up in a time of severe resource constraint. It seemed inevitable that only need defined as high dependency would receive service, even if the level of service might be higher than before. Fewer might mean better for some, but this would inevitably neglect the preventive function of community care. As she commented, social services departments were being asked to perform a tricky balancing act. They were expected to increase the involvement of users and carers, to begin to shift the balance of resources towards non-residential care, to develop further joint planning and commissioning (including GP fundholders) and to improve relationships with housing authorities. At the same time, the DH wanted a degree of 'steady state', in particular avoiding the market failure of private residential home providers and 'bed-blocking' in the NHS (Lewis, 1993, pp. 175–6). Certainly community care was no cheap option, as Titmuss had pointed out thirty years before. The logic of the community care plans also implied a course of action so far adopted by few authorities – joint planning and joint commissioning of services. The gap established in 1948 and widened subsequently, could be bridged; but few authorities had done so.

*Informal care*

As in the previous period, formal community care provision went hand in hand with informal care within the family. The continued reliance on informal care as part of community care was based on assumptions that a plentiful supply of female labour existed in the family and also that women were 'natural carers'. According to Hilary Graham, the burden of community care was placed primarily on women's shoulders (Graham, 1979). But in 1988, the first national survey of informal carers showed that among adults in Britain, 3.5 million women and 2.5 million men were looking after an elderly or disabled person. Men were caring as well as women. In most families, it was typically one person alone who took on the job of carer, with little or no support from formal agencies. Most carers were middle aged, with an increasing proportion elderly. The 1989 White Paper on community care acknowledged that carers' total input was greater than the combined inputs financed from central and local government (Hunter, 1993, p. 128). The real cost of family care was much greater than the cost of personal statutory social services.

Women have traditionally cared for other family members. But the nature of their role was changing. Research shows that most old people have a relative within half an hour travelling time, and improved communication since the 1950s – car and telephone – made contact easier even though increased mobility combined with decreased family size meant that elderly people often lived at a distance from relatives. In inner London, the proportion of elderly people who had a child living within five minutes' walk halved between the late 1950s and the late 1970s. Ties with neighbours were less close, more short-lived and compounded by racial divisions in some areas. The proportion of married working women rose sharply from the 1970s; but most research showed that family ties continued to be strong, even if the dependency of relatives was resented. During the 1970s unpaid caring began to be recognised through state benefits, but changes in the regulations in the 1980s made it more difficult for anyone to obtain the allowances, although further carers legislation was introduced in the 1990s. That the role of carers was recognised at all owed much to feminist analysis of the issue. Feminist studies of caring, by Janet Finch, Jane Lewis and others, pointed out that the assumption underlying social policy was that women do the caring. Finch and Groves argued that community care was fundamentally an equal opportunities issue; and Finch controversially argued for an extension in institutional care to alleviate this burden (Baldwin and Twigg, 1991). The feminist and earlier literature on carers by Townsend and others saw carers as victims and caring as a burden. But Thane (1990) has emphasised the reciprocity of relationships between old people and carers; only gradually did this balance alter. Women up to the age of 75 gave the community more than they took in terms of services. Assumptions about ageing and dependency were shown by historians to have greater complexity.

*Feminism and lay care*

This critique was part of a wider feminist debate round medicine and health care, which mounted a searching challenge to the role of biomedicine in general, arguing that medical science was actively sustaining a male-dominated gender order. This was part of the wider revolt against scientific medicine and the professional hegemony of doctors which has been discussed above. The role of lay care was central to this debate, which was inspired by international and especially American developments. From the late 1960s there was a more assertive approach to health matters on the part of women (Jones, 1994). The publication of the self-help text, *Our Bodies, Ourselves: A Health Book by and for Women*, by the Boston Women's Health Collective, originally published in 1971 in the US and republished in country specific versions elsewhere, spearheaded these developments. The British version was published in 1978. Women learnt more about their bodies so that they could exercise a greater control in the determination of their own health. Although the development of hospital-based childbirth pre- and post-war had been seen as a desirable development in terms of women's access to formal health care, there was a reaction against the high technology intervention this entailed. The medicalisation of childbirth was a key area of struggle. Historical accounts of childbirth and of the role of non-professional care played an important role in these debates. In 1985, the suspension of Wendy Savage, a consultant obstetrician in Tower Hamlets, appeared to stem in part from disapproval by male colleagues of her willingness to allow pregnant women autonomy in decision making about birth. These struggles were radical, but their emphasis on individual self-determination and autonomy also had echoes of the development of individualism in other areas of health policy. In health education and prevention, the emphasis changed to individual responsibility for health; and an emphasis on individual rights also marked AIDS activism.

*Lay care and community care*

This feminist focus on female autonomy and self-help was part of the general trend towards consumerism in health care. Consumerism and activism were closely linked and appealed to both ends of the political spectrum. Social scientists contributed to these issues in the 1960s and 70s when they began to study the patients' perception of illness and health (a tendency marked in historical studies as well). Stacey (1976), for example, argued that the patient was part of the process of health care. These analyses were paralleled by the activities of self-help groups, which continued to expand in this period. They were called the fourth estate in medicine (Allsop, 1995a, p. 254). Perhaps the clearest example in the 1980s in Britain and in the US came through the activities of self-help groups in relation to AIDS. Informal buddies provided lay care and support for people infected with HIV where initially formal statutory provision was non-existent. Networks of lay information and advice led to the widespread use of 'alternative' drugs without official approval and lay input was eventually sought in the design and management of clinical trials (Berridge, 1996). In Britain, groups such as the Terrence Higgins Trust defined AIDS and its care as an issue of individual human rights, continuing the emphasis on human rights begun in the mental health movement. In fact, there was some overlap in personnel between the two. By the mid-1990s, there were well over 800 self-help groups related to health in the UK. Groups typically lobbied for money to be spent on research, campaigned for truly informed consent before patients were involved in clinical trials, and offered advice to individual patients.

In other areas, specialist consumer organisations concerned with health care maintained a high profile. The Association of Community Health Councils and the Patients' Association campaigned on issues to safeguard patients' rights. The government drew on these activities for the model of the patient as consumer which informed the health service changes of the late 80s. Consumerism in the government model was rather different. It was exercised in a surrogate manner through the operation of the market and the intervention of GP fundholders. The implications of this are further discussed in the following section (pp. 84–5). The individualism and emphasis on 'rights' of the activist organisations focused increasingly on the contract in the 1990s. Patients were turning to the law to assert rights and duties within medicine.

*Lay beliefs*

AIDS demonstrated the persistence of long-held beliefs about health, illness and 'responsibility' for disease. Moral responsibility for infection had traditionally been a distancing mechanism by which populations ascribed forms of rationality to the randomness of epidemic disease. For all, 'good health' was a morally worthy state and illness discreditable, but the scientific discourse of medicine provided a major solution to the moral difficulties of illness. Once there was a medical diagnosis, then issues of individual responsibility and culpability were no longer relevant. The realm of lay beliefs about medicine and health, such a fruitful area of research for historians of earlier periods, has, as yet, been little studied from this perspective for the post-Second World War years. Historians have yet to realise the potential of oral history and of the data provided by the post-war social surveys. The work of sociologists and anthropologists provides an indication of the rich possibilities. The social anthropologist and general practitioner, Cecil Helman, showed how the 'folk model' of health and illness among patients in his general practice differed from the biomedical one, but was influenced by it and by practitioners' behaviour. His patients' distinction in types of illness between 'hot' and 'cold' and 'wet' and 'dry' was reminiscent of the medieval notions about health, illness and balance (Helman, cited in Stacey, 1988, pp. 149–50). Mildred Blaxter, working with Scottish working-class women, and Jocelyn Cornwell, researching in Bethnal Green, found that concepts of health varied according to immediate material circumstances. The extent to which people were dependent on their own physical labour, or could command their own daily lives and those of others, appeared to bear a relationship to what they thought about health. Both Blaxter and Cornwell found distinct differences in attitudes to and concepts of illness between older and younger people. Older people attached more significance to moral calibre and health, while younger ones placed more emphasis on external factors such as germs, viruses and social stress (Blaxter, 1990; Cornwell, 1984, p. 142). This may have represented a greater emphasis on moral self-control by those for whom professional health care had not always been an option before the NHS. Lay concepts varied from one class to another in ways which related to the material differences between the classes. Smoking was one example. A major cultural shift took place in the post-war period when the middle classes stopped smoking. Research on working-class women, and on inequalities and smoking, showed that smoking had different cultural connotations for the poorer sections of society. There its positive values were appreciated (Graham, 1987; Marsh and McKay, 1994). There was more concordance between the classes in views about inequality and health. This issue was rarely discussed, especially among those most likely to be exposed to 'disadvantaging environments' (Blaxter, 1997). Change over time was also important. As material circumstances changed and access to formal services improved, so lay beliefs also altered, as discussed in chapter 3 (Roberts, 1995). Medical innovations, for example the rise of hormone replacement therapy (HRT) in the management of the menopause, certainly affected lay views (Cornwell, 1984, p. 122). But medical hegemony was not accepted in areas which were considered 'non-medical' or in areas such as infant and child health where its jurisdiction was contested. Historical work on earlier periods has demonstrated that lay perceptions were inextricably interconnected with medical, but medical were also affected by the lay. They did not operate in separate realms of belief any more than they had done in the eighteenth century. Helman (1990) suggested that general practitioners colluded with the folk model. Work by Eade (in Marks and Worboys, 1997) showed how the lay beliefs of Bengali immigrants also interacted uneasily with those of expert opinion, whether Western or Islamic. Part of the reason for the persistence of such strong lay beliefs was the continuing importance of lay networks of information and advice. In the 1980s, the revival of the role of the community pharmacist was intended to build on the continued importance of informal advice and the sale of over the counter medicines (Anderson and Berridge, forthcoming). The rise of alternative medicine in a more formal and organised sense is discussed below.

## The health care division of labour

In the decades after 1974, health care occupations continued their shifts of boundary and status. A key issue was the promotion of alternative sources of power within health services in order to reduce the power of medical professionals. The rise of management within the NHS and the increased role of the 'patient as consumer' of health care in the 1980s seemed to herald the decline of medical autonomy. The rise of evaluation and of evidence-based medicine were research-based means of getting doctors to 'toe the line'. Whether medical power was in fact reduced is a matter for discussion in this section. The 'rise of professional society' since the late nineteenth century had included doctors and even what Perkin calls 'the bifurcation of the professional ideal' after the Second World War did not see them so easily dethroned from key expert status in health matters (Perkin, 1989).

### GPs and the rise of primary care

General practitioners continued to enhance their role and status, although with restrictions on the small business autonomy which had continued into the NHS in 1948. According to Lewis, primary care as it emerged in the 1970s was initially associated with public health. But the role of the GP subsequently became part of the concept. The international primary health care movement, enshrined in the 1978 Alma Ata Declaration sponsored by the World Health Organisation (WHO), expanded from its original Third

World focus into industrialised countries. In Britain, resear~ dings and reports (such as the 1981 Acheson Report on inner London GPs) showed that standards were low and could be improved. General practice was well placed to provide care in the community in particular with the increased policy emphasis on prevention of ill health. It fitted well with neo liberal Conservative values and began to fill the gap left by the removal of public health from its local community-based roots.

The role of team work and group practices continued to develop. In 1990, almost 60% of practices contained four or more doctors, about 30% had two or three and less than 10% were singlehanded. In 1952 almost 50% of GPs had been single-handed. The concept of the primary health care team replaced that of the single-handed GP. Between 1964 and 1977, the proportion of practices with an attached nurse increased from 12% to 84%. But the development of team work was not trouble free. Other staff in the primary care team worked to different goals and within different organisational structures. GPs in urban areas suffered from lack of overlap between the practice population and the area covered by the community staff.

GP autonomy came under scrutiny in the 1980s. Until the middle of that decade, there was virtually no knowledge of what went on in general practice or any control of prescribing. Control of the latter was the first demonstration of the government's willingness to risk political costs in order to bring financial costs under control. The introduction in November 1984 of the 'limited list' of drugs which GPs could prescribe took everyone by surprise and produced an 'eccentric alliance' in opposition between the medical profession, the pharmaceutical industry and the Labour Party. More control was to come. In 1990, despite intense GP opposition, the government imposed a new GP contract which for the first time made GPs more accountable to their Family Health Service Authorities (FHSAs). The regulation of GP activity was increased and GPs were required to provide more services. The method of payment was changed in order to provide incentives to carry out more work within the practice. Health promotion was a particular focus and money was available for health promotion clinics, a further demonstration of the developing GP role in what had traditionally been seen as the remit of public health. Further changes in the contract came in the 1990s when the health promotion funding

arrangements were changed so that clinics were no longer remuner-
ated (Florin, 1999). Lewis (1997) sees the 1990 contract as a
significant step in defining the core services which a GP had to
provide. In the 1960s, the GP had been approached by government
as a professional. In 1990, he or she was treated as a business
entrepreneur.

A parallel change was the introduction of GP fundholding in
1991. GPs could buy the whole range of services for their practice
populations. By 1995, fundholding practices covered one third of
the population. This was introduced despite professional opposition and calls for pilot projects to be implemented and evaluated. At
the time of writing, its effects were difficult to assess. There were
stories that fundholders' patients were receiving priority in access to
hospital care. Coulter (1995) saw its expansion as a significant shift
towards demand-led purchasing and away from a system based on
equitable allocation according to need. 'It is possible that this
trade-off between equity and efficiency will result in the hoped – for
quality improvements, although . . . it is by no means clear that
fundholding will turn out to be a more efficient system.' The rapid
development of GP fundholding also tipped the balance against
person-centred medicine, bringing to the fore the population-focused approach which had been an alternative tradition. However,
the GP practice population was not an appropriate one for all forms
of care (Lewis, 1997).

## Nursing

Management issues also affected nursing, and this period witnessed
both the 'rise of managerialism' and its decline so far as nursing was
concerned. The structural problems which beset the profession
continued. The 1974 reorganisation of the NHS following upon the
1966 Salmon Report on nursing gave nurse managers equal status
in planning with doctors and administrators. The male sector of the
nursing profession predominated in these posts out of all proportion
to the gender balance of nursing as a whole. Nurse management was
more immediately threatened than medicine by the Griffiths Report
of 1983. Nurses could apply for general management posts, but as
managers rather than as nurses. Few were appointed in great num-

bers at the higher levels, although they were appointed to other posts lower down the hierarchy.

This left nursing in the strategic dilemma which had affected it since the nineteenth century. Nurses could use the middle-management base to develop a higher management profile; they could also develop a more independent professional role. Throughout the 1980s, the 'professionalising' groups within nursing grew in power and prestige (Davey and Popay, 1993, p. 98). The Nursing, Midwifery and Health Visiting Act of 1979 generated a large professional base by including formerly separate nursing and health visiting sectors and increased professional control of entry through the independent UK Central Council. Through Project 2000, nurse education shifted towards an academic framework for training. Different work models allowed continuity of responsibility. Developments in the nursing hierarchy allowed clinical nursing consultants and emphasised the professional role. Enrolled Nurse training ended, to be reinvented, so some argued, as the health care assistant grade. Baly (1986) argued that nursing would always need some kind of two-tier system. The tension between the professional nurse and the handy woman role, with roots in the nineteenth century, continued.

## *Militancy and health care occupations*

The boundary between nurses' and doctors' work was a difficult one. Some doctors welcomed the extended role of the nurse, in particular where technical tasks, such as giving injections, could be delegated. Nurses were also playing a substantial role in the training of junior doctors. The lack of definition of these tasks was one factor behind increased militancy among junior and other doctors in the 1970s. The medical profession began to use the weapons of industrial warfare which had once been the monopoly of the trade unions. Militancy represented an acknowledgement that power was slipping away from the profession and towards other sectors in the NHS. Differentials between doctors and other health care workers were being squeezed, and so, too, were differentials between different sections of the medical profession. Junior doctors were particularly affected and their campaign in the 1970s over excessively long working hours was a high profile one including industrial action over pay in 1975. In what was also a grass roots rebellion against the BMA, junior doctors joined the Medical Practitioners' Union (MPU) which merged with the trade union ASTMS (now MSF) in 1970. The dispute led to an industrial-style contract which gave the junior doctors overtime payments, previously unthinkable for a 'professional' occupation. This salary increase led in its turn to an erosion of differentials with consultants and discontent on the part of the latter.

Consultants too became increasingly militant in the 1970s and the twin battle grounds with the Labour government over pay beds and the consultants' contract provided an explosive combination. The Labour government's commitment, at union insistence, was to phasing out pay beds and loading the consultant contract in favour of full-time work. Competition between the Hospital Consultants' and Specialists' Association and the BMA meant that they were engaged in a 'competition in militancy'.

In the event, the decline in pay beds proceeded slowly and the consultants' contract was never fully implemented. The new militancy within the NHS was not confined to medical professionals. The NHS workforce was huge – over 655,000 in 1968 (Webster, 1996, p. 824). The 1973 strike of ancillary workers brought results, but also destroyed the comfortable assumption that people working in the NHS did not take industrial action. Competition between the main unions involved – the Confederation of Health Service Employees (COHSE) and the National Union of Public Employees (NUPE), together with the Royal College of Nursing (RCN), which had both a professional and a trade union role, also increased the level of militancy.

This new assertiveness paid dividends. In the mid-1970s there was a rise of 25% in the costs of the NHS within which pay was the largest element. Average earnings for ancillary workers rose faster in percentage terms than those for doctors. But, as Stacey points out, in the mid-1980s there were still large differentials between different sectors of the health care workforce (Stacey, 1988, p. 188). In the 1990s Review Bodies on Pay revealed continued differentials. The highest-paid consultants earned well over twice as much as the highest-paid nurse, and a few were nearly able to double that with the top merit award.

## The rise of alternative medicine

Militancy among doctors could be seen as a response to an eroding power base. The threat came from a number of different directions. Pressure from alternative medicine practitioners was a professional threat which doctors had largely met by strategies both of incorporation (as with midwifery or the professions supplementary to medicine) or by exclusion, as with herbalism. From the 1970s what was then known as alternative medicine became more popular, along with the variety of alternative lifestyles. Alternative medicine was part of the attack on medical imperialism which marked much intellectual and historical commentary at the time and which has been discussed above. Attempts to count all the alternative practitioners in seven areas of Britain in 1981 estimated twelve such practitioners per 100,000 population (Seale, 1994, p. 18). Such practitioners in 1981 were therefore only a small fraction of the number in the professional sector. In February 1986, a *Which?* summary suggested that one in seven readers used alternative medicine, notably osteopaths. The British Holistic Medicine Association was founded in 1983. The changing stance of the BMA is indicated in its reports: *Alternative Medicine* (1986) was antagonistic in tone, but a further report on *Complementary Medicine: New Approaches to Good Practice* (1993) was, as its title suggests, less so. The strategy of incorporation was coming to the fore. There were moves towards formal registration and some GPs were receiving training in alternative therapies such as acupuncture and homeopathy. Many medically qualified doctors were becoming more interested in alternative medicine. One incentive may have been financial; the 1990 GP contract could pay for such interventions under the health promotion banner. Pharmacists, although not under the 'alternative' umbrella, were reconstituting their community and primary care image, in particular after the Nuffield Report of 1988. Psychological interventions in society proliferated. Traditional hospital psychiatry declined decisively in power and prestige but its decrease in institutional authority was accompanied by a 'seemingly endless intellectual expansion' (Micale and Porter, 1994, p. 13). The role of counselling received a particular impetus from the advent of AIDS; it became an automatic accompaniment to procedures such as HIV testing.

*Doctors and managers*

The other threat to medical autonomy came via the route of general management, introduced in 1984 in the wake of the Griffiths Report. The administrative strand of hospital structures moved centre stage as management combining two or three functions. This development was inspired by Griffiths' well-known phrase that 'if Florence Nightingale were carrying her lamp through the corridors of the NHS today she would almost certainly be searching for the people in charge' (quoted in Strong and Robinson, 1990, p. 22). The development of general management in the context of health service reorganisation has already been discussed in the first section of this chapter (pp. 61–7). Griffiths, schooled in Marks and Spencer, applied business models to the NHS, under the assumption that all organisations shared similar concerns with finance, structure and quality control. The role of the specialist provider of medical input was implicitly downgraded. General management and its introduction was soon followed by a host of other management changes. Performance indicators were developed for region and district; experimental methods were devised for assessing the costs of individual acts of medical care; a new health service training authority was created. But how far the power of the medical profession was reduced in practice remained initially debatable.

A further shift towards managerial influence came in the wake of the NHS reforms of the 1990s. The purchaser provider split led to a greater emphasis on outcomes rather than inputs. Evaluation of health care outcomes proliferated in order to aid purchasing decisions. Much more information became available to managers about the activities of doctors through performance indicators, resource management and medical audit. The traditional right of consultants to determine which patients were to be treated and how was also being challenged from another direction as well. Throughout the 1980s, there was a rising interest in techniques designed to measure the relative impact of different procedures in terms of the costs of different outcomes, a rise which gained greatest public attention in the concept of the QALY. It seemed that the technicians, the economists and the epidemiologists might be able to provide managers with tools for determining priorities. 'The ethical individualism of the medical profession (emphasising the doctor's responsibility to the individual patient) was increasingly being confronted by the utilitarianism of the economist and the epidemiologist (emphasising the impact of any individual decision on the population as a whole)' (Klein, 1995, p. 153). 'Evidence-based medicine' was a central concern of the 1990s, fuelled also by the establishment in 1991 of the NHS Research and Development initiative, which sought to bring research and its findings into a closer relationship with NHS practice (Black, 1997).

Managerial leverage over hospital doctors therefore became greater. But there were also changes in the balance of power within the medical profession; fundholding was shifting the balance of power from consultants to GPs. The ability of medical professionals to turn the new evaluative tools to their advantage should also not be forgotten. Klein distinguished between individual and collective professional autonomy. The individual autonomy of NHS consultants did seem to be shrinking. But it was being replaced by greater collective professional autonomy, which could be a strategic means of keeping managerial intervention at bay. One tool of collective professional autonomy, apart from those already discussed in the first section (pp. 64–5), was the increased focus on medical ethics. Local ethical committees expanded in order to regulate medical research. The role of medical ethicists and ethical codes gained significant prominence, providing the legal, philosophical and logical basis for the regulation of medical 'good behaviour'. This acceptance of ethics, although contested, was in contrast to the furore which had greeted Kennedy's Reith Lectures. He played a significant role in AIDS policy making in the 1980s; and ethical issues were important in medical responses at the local level as well (Berridge, 1996). These developments have been criticised (Karpf, 1988) for their failure to consider the socio-economic and political possibilities for and constraints upon asking the 'right' questions and arriving at the 'right' ethical conclusions. Cooter presents a historian's critique: 'for medical ethics to be historical would be to threaten this primary means to authority' (Cooter, 1995, p. 260). Nevertheless, medical ethics continued its rise in the 1990s even if some saw its protagonists as 'populist moralising politicians'.

Centrally, the role of medicine was modified, but remained important through representation on expert advisory committees. Different areas of health policy developed their own advisory committees and medical 'expert advisers' to the DH played an important role. Some of these committees were reconstituted in the 1980s to include a broader non-medical cross-section of opinion, but the medical expert committee still remained important, as was demonstrated by the role of the Expert Advisory Group on AIDS (EAGA) in the initial response to AIDS in the UK.

## Doctors and consumers

Changes in managerial and medical patterns of control did not lead to significant accretions of influence for lay or citizen representatives. The original criticism of the self-interest of professional groups had come from the Left rather than the Right in politics. But the democratic impetus was incorporated in more managerially focused changes (Perkin, 1989). Community Health Councils (CHCs) were of less importance; their members lost the right to attend meetings of DHAs. The latter also lost their local government nominees and trade union appointees. Self-governing NHS Trusts had to include 'community' representatives; but these, so research indicated, were mostly white, male and from business backgrounds. They were chosen and not elected. Yet at the same time, the concept of the NHS patient as the 'consumer' of health care became ever stronger through the Citizens' and Patients' Charters and through the belief that the market in health care would be responsive to individual needs. There were moves to make more information available to patients so that they could be more involved in aspects of their own care. Various new technical means attracted much attention as ways of ascertaining collective views on health care. 'Citizens' juries' and 'focus groups' were fashionable. Much lay and patient involvement in practice came through proxies, such as managers and fundholding GPs. When consultation was carried out many NHS managers and professionals did not have the skills to listen to what lay people were saying. Some were quite capable of disregarding what they did not like to hear. Popay and Williams concluded that 'Effective lay participation within the NHS will only be achieved when there is a more democratic structure within the health care system' (Popay and Williams, 1994, p. 93). The closer alliance of local and health authorities in the provision of community care also in theory could lead to greater democratic involvement in health care matters through local government political structures and the ballot box. By the mid-1990s, however, there were few signs that these were political issues at the local level. 'Patient' or 'consumer power' within the NHS was exercised in a surrogate manner, or in a form of atomised individualism through legal procedures. The focus on human rights and self-help which has already been discussed was also expressed through increased patient willingness to sue for damages. The idea of the contract, which underpinned the social welfare changes of the 1980s, also had its impact on the power and role of the patient as consumer.

## The public's health and public health: variations and inequalities

Public health as a formal profession, as a concept and a set of beliefs about the health of the population, underwent considerable change during these years. The medical wing of public health once more attempted to reinvent its role, while a broader public health constituency emerged with a clearly defined agenda around 'lifestyle' issues. Criticism of the lifestyle approach came from both ends of the political spectrum. Inequalities, overlooked in the focus on the individual, seemed to be re-emerging as an issue in the 1990s. This section will also look at the 'balance sheet' of the health of the population in that decade, after fifty years of the NHS.

### Changes in the public health profession

Public health as a formal medical profession had been at a crossroads at the end of the 1960s, with the old role of the MoH in the local authorities on the point of disappearing. The new role in the reorganised NHS was yet to be established. Many in the public health profession welcomed the new changes which offered the apparently tangible advantages, to a medically based profession, of incorporation within mainstream specialist services within the hospital, and of consultant status. The establishment of the Faculty of

Community Medicine in 1972 and changes in public health training both emphasised the reorientation of this medical subgroup
towards specialist status and towards the concept of medical administration, seen as giving the MoH a more central place in the
medical care system. The 1972 Hunter report on medical administration had envisaged the community physician as the crucial link
person in the reformed health service.

But in the event, these initial high hopes were dashed. The 1974
reorganisation created posts at region, area and district levels. The
removal of the area tier in 1982 simplified relationships, but also
resulted in a greater polarisation between the management and
'specialist/adviser' strands within community medicine. There was
disillusionment and fully 20% of public health doctors took early
retirement in 1982. The change from consensus management to
clearer lines of accountability after the 1984 Griffiths Report
eroded the role of the community physician even further. As Lewis
points out, the position of the community physician was subject to
serious conflicts in terms both of the relationship with other members of the medical profession and the nature of the primary responsibility, whether for the management of health services or for
the analysis of health problems and needs (Lewis, 1986, p.135).
Although initially the concept of primary care meant public health
rather than general practice, the partnership with the local community which had characterised the role of the MoH was lost.
There was also unease within the profession about managing
health services rather than analysing broader health problems. The
revived role of general practice also (as discussed in chapter 3)
provided an alternative community-based location for activities
which had been traditional to the MoH.

The apparent revival of 'formal' public health in the 1980s left
most of these issues unresolved. The specific impetus was a traditional one, through the threat of communicable disease. Outbreaks of salmonella at Stanley Royd Hospital in 1984 and
Legionnaires disease at Stafford in the following year highlighted
the shortage of infectious disease specialists. The advent of AIDS
as a potentially epidemic disease in the mid-1980s added an extra
urgency and provoked a high level crisis (Berridge, 1996). An
inquiry was held into the future of the public health function,
chaired by Sir Donald Acheson, the Chief Medical Officer, who

was himself a public health epidemiologist. The resultant Acheson Report (1988), strongly influenced by the history of public health in England, made a determined effort to upgrade the status of public health. It proposed the appointment of regional Directors of Public Health, the revival of annual public health reports (abandoned in 1974 with the demise of the MoH) and the development of more intersectoral collaboration, rather than the exclusive focus on health services. But the Acheson Report placed prime emphasis on the maintenance of parity with other medical specialisms. The speciality was to be known as 'public health medicine', but the independent and politically contentious watchdog role was avoided. The strong medical emphasis precluded the likelihood of an effective intersectoral approach. The importance of epidemiology in giving the speciality scientific legitimacy was emphasised as it had been by Ryle in the 1940s or by Morris in the 1960s and 70s.

The new Directors of Public Health and their staff began to develop a new empire around health education and promotion, together with the measurement of health need and resource allocation. The health service reforms brought public health doctors (and some non-medical public health personnel) a role as the purchasers of health services. The 'specialist administrator' role rather than that of 'public watchdog' predominated. Even in central government policy making, public health did not fulfil the initial expectations raised by AIDS and it had little impact on health promotion issues in primary care (Berridge, 1996; Florin, 1999).

## Changes in the concept: the new public health constituency

The formal medical public health profession was but one section, albeit an important one, of a broader public health/health promotion constituency which developed during these years. This had as an organising belief the association of public health with changes in individual lifestyle. The origin of this approach in the smoking issue has already been discussed (chapter 3). In the 1970s the idea of prevention as an individual issue was carried further both nationally and internationally. The 1974 Lalonde Report, *A New Perspective on the Health of Canadians*, was influenced by the 'McKeown thesis' (already discussed) that overall standards of population health bore less relationship to medical intervention than to standards of diet and overall standards of living (Leichter, 1991). There were similar reports in other countries. The British version was an initial consultative document *Prevention and Health: Everybody's Business*, published in 1976, followed by a White Paper, *Prevention and Health*, in the following year. Despite the efforts of some academic social medicine protagonists to insert more social context, the report adopted an individual lifestyle approach. Much emphasis was placed on the use of health education. Nevertheless, the work of the Health Education Council remained subject to both budgetary and political constraints, and to tensions in the relationship between Chairmen and Directors of the Council. There were rapid changes of personnel. In Scotland, the Scottish Health Education Group established more of an independent reputation.

The term 'health promotion' began to be used in the late 1970s, originating in these various policy documents. In the early 1980s, the Health for All by the Year 2000 strategy of the World Health Organisation (HFA) established targets which were used by individual countries and also gave the term 'health promotion' greater currency. There remained, however, some confusion about what this term really meant.

Traditional public health activities such as vaccination were less important in the public eye, with low acceptance rates in the 1970s for measles and rubella campaigns. The issue of whooping cough vaccine safety (some children had been brain damaged by the vaccine) made the public warier than ever of this strategy, and the Association of Parents of Vaccine Damaged Children waged a high-profile campaign in the 70s and 80s (Webster, 1996, p. 681). The new individualisation of health issues continued. 'Single issues' were highlighted rather than a broader concern for social context. Individual action could remedy health ills; the role of women as mothers was given special attention. These ideas were a natural reaction to a period when scientific, high technology medicine had been centre stage. They drew on long-standing beliefs about health which stressed the value of a healthy regimen – diet, exercise and moderate living – and intermingled powerfully with the lay beliefs about moral responsibility for health and healthy living which have been discussed in the previous section. The focus on the individual was also, almost paradoxically, set within a population-based perspective which denied the importance of the individual. This was the 'prevention paradox' enunciated by the epidemiologist Geoffrey Rose (Rose, 1992). Only a small proportion of 'high risk' individuals would go on to develop the threatened disease and a high proportion of those who did, showed no risk factors. The risk potential of the group was no predictor for the individual. Nevertheless, public health strategies stressed population-based approaches, founded on the premises of epidemiology and the concept of relative risk in order to achieve these individual aims. This epitomised the rise of the belief in statistical correlation rather than reproducible experimentation.

This new public health/health promotion constituency stressed population-based interventions, taxation as a public health tool, with a focus on control of advertising and on public information and mass advertising to achieve objectives. The media techniques which had originated in the 1960s were further developed and the Health Education Council began to use 'modern' techniques of persuasion. The advertising agency, Saatchi and Saatchi, first gained a reputation through the campaigns it mounted for the HEC in the 1970s.

The smoking and alcohol issues provided examples of this approach. Baggott (1990) has shown how a previously fragmented 'alcohol lobby', diverse groups, each drawing attention to one particular aspect of the problem, unified in the 1970s round the level of alcohol consumption. The Ledermann theory of alcohol consumption, which argued that changes in the level of alcohol consumption by society as a whole had a bearing on the level of its alcohol problems, provided a unifying concept for a revived 'alcohol misuse lobby'. The DHSS Advisory Committee on Alcoholism was an important catalyst in presenting an agenda which focused round health education, taxation and advertising, with a lessening emphasis on specialist treatment.

A similar process was at work for smoking. After the first Royal College of Physicians Report in 1961, the objectives of policy had been to develop safer smoking products as well as to encourage smokers to stop. The higher taxation option was not universally accepted in public health circles because it would bear more harshly upon the poorer sections of society who were perhaps more reliant on their smoke. But these attitudes changed in the 1970s and a harsher public health line developed. 'Safer cigarettes' and the introduction of non-tobacco material proved to be an expensive debacle, thus undermining the safer smoking option. But the public health constituency, arguing through the 1971 and 1977 RCP reports also developed a policy agenda which stressed, as for alcohol, higher taxation, health education, a ban on advertising and mass media techniques of persuasion (Berridge, 1998). In the early 1980s, this new public health constituency coalesced round the concept of 'passive smoking', which stressed a risk to all rather than, as before, just to the individual smoker. Population-based strategies were again the focus. But 'passive smoking', emphasising as it did, the environmental risk as well as the individual one, also presaged a revival of environmentalism within public health, which would gather pace in the 1980s (Berridge, 1999).

Diet and nutrition also claimed a higher profile in public terms from the late 1970s. The publication of the NACNE (National Advisory Committee on Nutrition Education) guidelines in 1983, followed the next year by a second report from the Committee on the Medical Aspects of Food Policy (COMA) drew out the relationship between diet and heart disease. These led to health education campaigns against fats, such as 'Look After Your Heart' and 'Heartbeat Wales'. As Murcott points out, the healthy eating movement gained momentum – but few were sure what healthy eating really was (Murcott, 1994; Holmes, 1993). Cornwell's research also demonstrated a fair amount of popular opposition to health campaigns on eating habits.

These issues, as well as other 'single issues' in the 'health promotion' arena, were also more than a matter simply for public health. They were the subject of conflicting interdepartmental priorities, not least relating to the maintenance of industrial, fiscal and trade interests. A report on alcohol, for example, produced by the Central Policy Review Staff of the Cabinet Office in the 1970s and recommending a broad interdepartmental approach to the reduction of alcohol consumption, was never officially published. Instead, the government produced a much milder document, *Drinking Sensibly*, in 1981, which took a less comprehensive stance and did not challenge the alcohol industry. A similar interdepartmental examination of anti-smoking measures had also gone unpublished in 1971.

## Criticism of public health

Attacks on the 'health promotion' model came from both ends of the political spectrum. The 'radical right' represented in the Social Affairs Unit and elsewhere argued that health promotion was part of a nanny state which sought to regulate the population through fear of 'risks' which were scientifically contentious (Le Fanu, 1994). The public health constituency was also uncertain whether 'high-risk' or 'population-based' strategies should be adopted. Diet and heart disease was one contentious area, where the debate was highlighted by the issue of screening for cholesterol (Calnan, 1991). Some evidence appeared to point away from population-based strategies to lower cholesterol levels and towards a focus on 'high-risk' individuals. Screening for cholesterol, it was argued, could be an expensive waste of time. Alongside the attack on the 'population' approach established in the 70s and 80s came a revived emphasis on social class. Class as well as lifestyle was an important predictor of health. It was pointed out, for example, that the relationship between smoking and heart disease made no allowance for social class; smokers tended to be in lower social classes, in itself a risk factor for coronary heart disease. Blaxter's research (1990) also showed that circumstances, with social support, carried more weight for outcome than behaviour. There was a greater questioning of campaigns which solely targeted individual 'risk factors' such as smoking and a realisation that the high taxation option for smoking control had implications in terms of penalising the poorest sections of the population who continued to smoke.

## Whither public health – over to primary care?

In the 1980s came the development of what became known as the 'new public health' which purported to marry the twin objectives of personal prevention and a growing reawakening of interest in environmental matters. The environment was seeing something of a revival. This was associated with the WHO's Health for All (HFA) strategy, adopted by the European office of WHO in 1984. The organisation's Healthy Cities initiative had an impact on a number of countries. Some local authorities in England established local strategies for promoting health which addressed environmental issues such as traffic pollution and leisure facilities. The WHO's emphasis on target setting was later subsumed into the *Health of the Nation* document. The emergence of the 'sustainable development' movement in the 1980s largely affected developing countries. But after the 1987 Brundtland Commission Report, *Our Common Future*, and the 1992 Rio conference on the environment, came a further series of local initiatives on the model of the earlier Healthy Cities. Local Agenda 21, one of these, again brought the local authorities back into considering broader public and environmental matters. The possibilities for greater intersectoral collaboration were there with this issue as they were with community care (see above). In the 1990s the emphasis in a number of different policy areas (illicit drugs was one, the control of public drinking another) on the concept of 'community safety' brought issues of health, the environment and legal regulation at the local level on to the policy agenda.

The origin of these issues also emphasised another change: the growing importance of the international and especially the European dimension to public health policy issues. WHO had been important in the post-war period in defining international health responses, and Europe was a growing centre of influence. Webster (1996, p. 756) notes that EEC proposals, for example, for tax harmonisation for alcohol, for the control of lead emissions in petrol and for control of tobacco advertising, caused the British government to produce policy responses more swiftly than it might otherwise have done. This impetus gathered pace after the Maastricht Treaty of 1991 specifically included public health.

Despite this broadening remit at both the national and the international levels, there were long-standing tensions in the remit of public health. The public health community was much broader by the 1980s; and environmental health officers, health promotion officers and GPs all maintained that they, too, had a role in formulating healthy public policies. However, the official public health response remained a medicalised one and attempts to broaden the Faculty of Public Health Medicine were largely failures. Arguably primary care and the pivotal role of the GP were to an extent taking over the community role of the old public health physician. GPs were holding statistics on their practice populations, but the primary care approach was therapeutically oriented despite attempts to inject health promotion into the GP contract.

## The inequalities debate

One issue which was largely off the agenda throughout the 1970s and 80s was that of inequalities and health and the relationship between class and health. The most notorious case of non-publication of a politically contentious health report was the attempt by the incoming Conservative government in 1980 to restrict the circulation of the Black Report, *Inequalities in Health*. The circulation of 260 duplicated copies of the typescript on the Friday before the August Bank Holiday was initially a successful strategy for containing discussion of the issue. But ultimately it only attracted more media attention. The report was published as a best-selling paperback as well as stimulating wide debate about the continuing issue of inequalities. A follow-up report, *The Health Divide*, produced in 1987 under the auspices of the Health Education Council and its campaigning Director, Dr David Player, suffered a similar fate. The Chairman of the HEC, Sir Brian Bailey, cancelled the launch press conference an hour before it was due to take place and the authors of the report had to hold the conference on the pavement outside. The resultant media coverage was massive. AIDS provided the ostensible reason for the removal of Player and the reorganisation of the HEC as the new Health Education Authority (HEA) (Berridge, 1996).

The issue of inequalities contained within it the dimensions of environment, housing and social class, an essentially political project for public health which was largely off the government's agenda in the 1980s (Townsend and Davidson, Whitehead, 1988). MacIntyre (1997) has surveyed both the political dimensions of the issue in the 1980s and the considerable research debate which it generated. At least forty articles a year on average were published on the subject in Britain during the decade. The debate, as MacIntyre notes, concentrated on these disparities and their explanation rather than the policy prescriptions the report put forward. She comments that its policy focus on education, disability and health damaging behaviours suggests that it did not take as hard a structural line on the origin of inequalities as the subsequent debate implied.

In policy terms, the issue was recognised, but was in no sense a priority. The publication of the government White Paper on *The Health of the Nation* in 1992, recalled, in its title, the earlier fin de siècle concern with health as a national resource. The document set targets for key areas such as sexual health and coronary heart disease. It was welcomed, but also criticised for avoiding contentious issues such as unemployment and health which were perhaps less amenable to target setting. In the 1990s, inequalities did begin to re-emerge in policy-making circles, although under the rubric of 'variations in health'. It was initially unclear who would carry this forward as a campaigning issue. Bartley argued that the 'incorporation' of public health doctors in reformed health service machinery meant that they had dropped their interest in the issue (Bartley, 1994). The election of a Labour government in 1997 brought heightened interest in public health and the issue of inequalities was explicitly addressed in a Green Paper.

But what was happening to the health of the nation at the end of the century – and fifty years after the foundation of the NHS? The Black Report, using data from the early 1970s, had concluded,

most recent data show marked differences in mortality rates between the occupational classes, for both sexes and at all ages ... a class gradient can be observed for most causes of death, being particularly steep in the case of diseases of the respiratory system . . . available data on chronic sickness tend to parallel those on mortality ... the lack of improvement and in some cases deterioration of the health experience of the unskilled and semi-skilled manual classes (class V and IV) relative to class I throughout the 1960s and early 1970s is striking . . . inequalities exist also in the utilisation of health services, particularly and most worryingly of the preventive services . . . France, like Britain and most other countries considered (though apparently not Sweden) shows significant class and regional inequalities in health.                                    (Townsend *et al.* 1988, pp. 198–9)

By the mid-1990s, at the research level, knowledge of the extent of inequalities had been refined. It was clear that social class gradients in mortality, morbidity and growth were to be found in all industrialised countries. There was some evidence of increasing inequalities in health in Britain through the 1980s; there were increasing inequalities in mortality between the 1971 and 1981 censuses. There was evidence of a lack of decline, or increase in mortality among the poorer groups. This was in a period when mortality rates in general had steadily declined.

There seemed little doubt in the mid-1990s that inequalities in health still existed and that the gap between classes (or social groups) had in some cases widened rather than narrowed. But the explanation for all this remained controversial. The work of Barker's group, using historical data, posited the hypothesis that patterns of adult health and mortality were influenced by biological programming in utero or early infancy. This line of explanation implicitly downgraded both environmental and behavioural approaches to health (as well as continuing the historic focus on the responsibility of mothers). MacIntyre notes that the debate between the 'early life programming' theorists and the 'continued social disadvantage' school is currently one of the most active areas of the inequalities debate in Europe. Other, more sociologically oriented, work looked at the 'life course' nature of inequalities; inequalities seem to be less manifest in adolescence on some measures of mortality and morbidity.

Inequalities persisted and even widened. But was the population healthier? Here the position was equivocal. Mortality continued to improve and there had been striking gains since the 1970s. Between 1970 and 1972 and 1990 and 1992, both men and women gained an extra three years of life expectancy at age 15 and an extra year at age 65 – but there was no comparable increase in the number of years of healthy life. Illness in the population in general had not reduced in that period. The increase in the very elderly continued – and this could be a burden or a boost for society dependent on health in old age. The greatest improvements came in the under 10 age group but there were also substantial improvements in the 45–54 band. Men, rather than women, fared better in the 45–74-year-old reduction in mortality (Charlton and Murphy, 1997, pp. 17–30). Infectious disease mortality continued its decline, with the proportion of deaths from cancer and circulatory disease increasing, especially among men (Charlton and Murphy, 1997). Perinatal and maternal mortality rates fell, the first by 80% since 1950, the latter by 91%. Britain had achieved lower rates sooner and other countries caught up. Other indicators were also positive. The numbers of adults without teeth had significantly reduced – two-fifths of adults had no teeth in 1968, but only one fifth in 1988. Some health-related behaviours like smoking had reduced considerably since the 1970s, but with little change among men and women aged 16–24 in the last ten years, and with continuing class gradients. Levels of physical activity remained static. The population was taller and heavier – but obesity was the problem. Despite this change of focus, there were still groups in the population who ate less, or less well, in particular those in receipt of benefits and their children. Some research showed ethnic differences, with black single-parent families eating more nutritious meals than their white counterparts (Charlton and Quaife, 1997). It was difficult to avoid agreement with Dunnell's (1997) conclusion that some things were better, some things worse, and some things about the same.

# 5
# Conclusion

All historical work is defined by the present. With an end date in the 1990s and with many areas of post-war health experience and policy as yet unresearched, the conclusions to be drawn here must be even more contingent than is generally the case. This book has encompassed health at three levels – patterns of health, formal health services and areas of health policy, distinct from services. The conclusion will touch on all three. The focus in this book is on the British experience. How did Britain compare with patterns in other industrialised countries and their health care systems? Gray (1993) has pointed out that some issues affected all countries in the post-war period. The long period of unprecedented economic growth after 1948, accompanied by expansion of welfare provision, was interrupted by the oil price rise of 1973, which led to deteriorating economic growth and welfare policies under increasing strain. The way in which Britain coped with those pressures differed significantly from other countries. Gray's calculations show that in all OECD countries, formal health care continued to take an increased share of GDP. But most of that real increase in spending was a reflection of individuals making more use of health services. Population change and the rise in the proportion of the elderly were of relatively minor importance. Rates of use had risen for a variety of different reasons; in part through the role of technology, in part because of increased expectations (Gray, 1993, pp. 181–2). This pattern of growth slowed in all countries in the late 70s and 80s. Where did Britain fit in? Its pattern of expenditure was similar, but it fell further and further behind the OECD average from the 1970s. A country's national income is typically a predictor of expenditure on health systems; but Britain, with a similar national income to Italy or

Spain, devoted a smaller proportion of GDP to health. Only Greece of OECD countries, spent less of its GDP on health. The UK's total health care spending was one quarter below the EC average (Allsop, 1995b, p. 105).

The British system, still primarily tax funded rather than insurance based, had been able to hold down costs more effectively. This parsimonious reality was far from the public image of the system. Despite all the reorganisation and the investigation of the NHS from different political directions, the service had remained a tax-funded one, and this made health issues intensely political. The high profile of the British system had unfortunately been long accompanied by a quite undeserved reputation for high costs and this image had in part fuelled the drive for reorganisation, efficiency and cost cutting in the late 1980s. Despite the supposed radicalism of the 1980s/90s Conservative government, the essential basis of the system had remained. So, too, had the issue of cost containment. Evidence of underfunding from the start was there – but increasing the NHS budget was not really on any political agenda. The service had always had clear deficiencies – there was lack of coordination in the tripartite organisation of GPs, hospital and community services, little democratic input and the service was dominated professionally by doctors and, in structural terms, by the hospital sector. But the NHS, in its classic period up to the 1990s reorganisation, had offered an exceptional model of universal access at relatively low cost, energised by an ethos of public service. Technology, for example through hip replacement, had offered clear benefits. The service offered particular gains for women, who had only limited care under the insurance-based system. No other country, so its Chief Executive declared in 1998, had found a better answer.[1]

In the 1990s much changed. The service presented more of a 'patchwork' as the result of the NHS 'reforms'. Central control of finance had increased, but responsibility had been pushed out to the localities. Administrative costs soared. Some commentators argued that the NHS was no longer a *national* service at all, and that there had been a return to the overlapping confusion of the interwar

---

[1] Debate 7 January 1998 at the King's Fund on the past, present and future of the NHS (see p. 17 n.1)

years. But central control of finance had not operated then to the same degree. Such oscillations between centralism and local autonomy had long characterised the British health care system. Services in England and Wales and Scotland were separately administered, resulting in different and historically determined patterns of policy change. The changes of the 1990s brought on the one hand greater local fragmentation together with an apparently greater degree of central control of the service through the NHSME. Even the centre was fragmented, with the DH and the NHSME as alternative power bases. The diversity of forms of care through the 'mixed economy' of care was greater than ever. Some argued that the NHS was becoming an acute service only, rather than one that catered for the general health problems of the population. There was a dramatic fall in beds in the 1980s and early 1990s and the principle of universality was undermined (table 5).

The role of the medical profession also had changed. Allsop (1995b, p. 121) sees interesting parallels in the running battles between the medical profession and the incoming Labour government in the 1940s, and the profession's struggle with Conservative politicians over the NHS reforms and the GP contract in the 1990s. The fiftieth anniversary of the NHS in 1998 was certainly, as Julian Tudor Hart commented, no celebration of a 'golden wedding' between the NHS and the profession.[2] Professional issues were no longer left untouched. But how far the role of professionals had really been reduced remains uncertain. At the local level, the doctor/manager dichotomy was more complex than it seemed; many doctors were managers. Issues of rationing and priority setting were discussed more openly, with input from the disciplines of economics, ethics and epidemiology, rather than the covert and paternalistic professional system which had operated before. Hospital consultants were more accountable. Central expert committees widened their membership to include a range of non-medical personnel. The post-war period demonstrates clear changes in the balances of power both within the profession, between specialist hospital doctor and GP, and between the specialist profession and other forms of technical expertise.

Politics were an inextricable part of the health policy scene, even

---

[2] Ibid.

if, as Webster notes, the results achieved by governments of different political complexions were often indistinguishable. This book started with reference to political theories which could inform the study of the history of health policy. 'Structured pluralism' with governments the strongest force operated in the post-war period. Lowe (1993) favours a theory of incrementalism in welfare policy in general and Klein (1995) proposes a kind of techno-bureaucratic consensus which has had particular influence on health policy making. The assessment must depend largely on which areas of policy, at what times, and at what levels are under discussion. Webster (1996) rightly emphasises the importance of politicians in the health policy-making process, drawing attention to the role of relatively unsung post-war Ministers of Health (such as Walker-Smith) as well as to those such as Powell and Crossman more conventionally associated with the role. Politicians could have a decisive influence, in particular when in alliance with civil servants, as aspects of the AIDS crisis in the mid-1980s illustrate. The alliance between the Department of Health and the Treasury, when it has existed, has also been important for funding.

But political input is not all. There are also areas of policy making where the influence of politicians has been decisive, but also sporadic. Other influences can come to bear in the interim periods. Policy making is often a question of implementation and here, too, bureaucratic and pressure group influence can be considerable. The idea of 'policy communities' operating to determine particular policy lines does not therefore downgrade political influence. The organisation of the NHS has always had a high political priority in the post-war period. But not all health policy making is specifically service related and here there are areas where such communities have developed policy with only intermittent political intervention. Illicit drugs and alcohol are particular examples, where strong links developed between outside interests and civil servants in the DH.

These interpretations seem to support the notion of a 'post-war consensus', where shared priorities over policy operated until shattered by the advent of the Conservative government in the 1980s and 90s. This interpretation is debatable, as the survey of contributions in this text has shown. It may also be open to further debate even in relation to the 'Thatcher revolution'. AIDS policy making in the mid- to late 1980s, for example, shows the traditions of liberal consensual policy making continuing at the height of the 'Thatcher revolution' and over an issue which would seem to have been well suited to its emphasis on family values (Berridge, 1996). The impression of fundamental change is central to the 1980s, but commentators have also noted continuities in other areas of health policy as well.

Some issues were perennial. Demand continued to increase. Access and equity were not dealt with, and these issues became more urgent with the fragmentation of services. The issue of accountability also remained unresolved. The European insurance-based systems, although less cost effective, had ensured greater public responsiveness. Despite efforts to improve information systems in the NHS in the 1980s, information about how the system worked remained inadequate. The 'consumer revolution' of the 1990s, deriving from the activism of the 1970s, barely disguised the lack of democratic input into health decision making. Poor performance was still tolerated. In 1998, the service was commissioning its first ever survey of what patients thought of the quality of the service they received. Individualisation was the watchword across a variety of health arenas, from prevention to consumer protection; and the contractual relationship appeared to have replaced the influence of democratic procedures. Community care lay within the purview of local government, but health policies were essentially depoliticised at that level. Discussion of health priorities was rarely a political issue at the local level, unless the issue was one of hospital closure.

Integrating services and crossing boundaries were on the agenda by the late 1990s. The health and social service disjuncture was increasingly discussed and there was awareness of the relevance of the environmental, housing, food and agricultural dimensions to health policy. The impact of a Labour government on what Webster (1998) has called a 'disjointed and atomised internal market' remains to be observed. The impact of devolution in Scotland and Wales appeared to offer a greater opportunity than in England for systems to integrate the NHS with services administered by local government. But other commentators argued that the idea of 'seamless services' was unattainable. Local authority, GP and hospital services had very different historical roots. What was needed was perhaps closer 'stitching of the seams'.[3] Boundary realignment lies in the future – and much of the post-war health scene remains to be researched (Bridgen and Lowe, 1998). Lay attitudes to health; the development of health policy outside formal service provision; the histories of a whole range of areas from health education to the diffusion of new technology need research which can feed into an understanding of the bases of the present. Traditionally, the NHS and British health policy has been compared with the US health care system. But histories of health care in Europe also provide significant contrasts. Why, asks Lowe, did Britain, with its strong tradition of insurance-based health care, adopt a tax-funded system in the 1940s when France veered towards insurance? Why, when the British system was one of the most economical in Europe, was health care reform carried through here in the 1980s while the expensive French system stayed unreformed? Comparing cross-nationally within Europe could be an illuminating perspective in the post-war histories which remain to be researched and written.

[3] J. Lewis, 'Making recent community and primary care policy', lecture, LSHTM, 1997.

# Tables

Table 1 *Age-specific trends in mortality, 1941–1994*

Rates per 10,000 population

| Year | <1 | 1–4 | 5–14 | 15–19 | 20–4 | 25–34 | 35–44 | 45–54 | 55–64 | 65–74 | 75–84 | 85 & over |
|---|---|---|---|---|---|---|---|---|---|---|---|---|
| *Males* | | | | | | | | | | | | |
| 1941–5 | 560 | 37 | 14 | 29 | 56 | 42 | 48 | 99 | 231 | 517 | 1,216 | 2,261 |
| 1951–5 | 300 | 12 | 6 | 9 | 14 | 14 | 27 | 79 | 225 | 546 | 1,267 | 2,659 |
| 1961–5 | 230 | 9 | 4 | 9 | 11 | 11 | 25 | 74 | 217 | 540 | 1,213 | 2,532 |
| 1971–5 | 190 | 7 | 4 | 9 | 9 | 10 | 22 | 72 | 201 | 511 | 1,151 | 2,371 |
| 1981–5 | 110 | 5 | 3 | 8 | 8 | 9 | 17 | 57 | 174 | 452 | 1,035 | 2,208 |
| 1991–4 | 74 | 4 | 2 | 6 | 8 | 9 | 17 | 43 | 132 | 373 | 914 | 1,966 |
| *Females* | | | | | | | | | | | | |
| 1941–5 | 440 | 33 | 12 | 23 | 28 | 25 | 33 | 64 | 140 | 360 | 935 | 2,066 |
| 1951–5 | 230 | 10 | 4 | 6 | 9 | 11 | 21 | 49 | 118 | 331 | 924 | 2,220 |
| 1961–5 | 180 | 8 | 3 | 4 | 5 | 7 | 18 | 44 | 106 | 298 | 836 | 2,067 |
| 1971–5 | 150 | 6 | 2 | 4 | 4 | 6 | 16 | 44 | 102 | 264 | 745 | 1,889 |
| 1981–5 | 90 | 4 | 2 | 3 | 3 | 5 | 12 | 36 | 96 | 241 | 644 | 1,759 |
| 1991–4 | 58 | 3 | 1 | 3 | 3 | 4 | 11 | 27 | 78 | 216 | 578 | 1,518 |

*Source*: Taken from Charlton and Murphy, 1997.

Table 2 *Death rates by disease, 1951–1994*

| Year | All causes | I Infectious diseases | II Neoplasms | III Endocrine | IV Blood | V Mental disorders | VI Nervous system | VII Circulatory system | VIII Respiratory system |
|---|---|---|---|---|---|---|---|---|---|
| *Persons* | | | | | | | | | |
| 1951 | 100.0 | 3.6 | 16.0 | 1.0 | 0.4 | 0.2 | 1.1 | 48.4 | 15.3 |
| 1971 | 100.0 | 0.6 | 20.8 | 1.2 | 0.3 | 0.3 | 1.1 | 51.7 | 13.1 |
| 1991 | 100.0 | 0.4 | 25.5 | 1.8 | 0.3 | 2.4 | 2.1 | 45.9 | 11.1 |
| 1994 | 100.0 | 0.6 | 25.6 | 1.3 | 0.3 | 1.5 | 1.6 | 43.8 | 14.7 |

| Year | IX Digestive system | X Genito-urinary system | XI Maternal mortality | XII Skin | XIII Musculo-skeletal | XIV Congenital anomalies | XV Perinatal period | XVI Symptoms ill defined | XVII Injury and poisoning |
|---|---|---|---|---|---|---|---|---|---|
| *Persons* | | | | | | | | | |
| 1951 | 2.8 | 2.5 | 0.1 | 0.1 | 0.3 | 0.8 | 1.9 | 1.8 | 3.6 |
| 1971 | 2.6 | 1.4 | 0.0 | 0.1 | 0.5 | 0.8 | 1.1 | 0.6 | 4.0 |
| 1991 | 3.2 | 1.1 | 0.0 | 0.2 | 1.0 | 0.3 | 0.4 | 0.9 | 3.0 |
| 1994 | 3.4 | 1.2 | 0.0 | 0.2 | 0.6 | 0.2 | – | 1.4 | 2.9 |

*Source:* Taken from Charlton and Murphy, 1997.

Table 3 *Infant mortality in Europe, 1970–1994*

| IMR | United Kingdom | Sweden | France | Italy | Spain |
|---|---|---|---|---|---|
| 1970 | 18.49 | 11 | 15.14 | 29.55 | 20.78 |
| 1971 | 17.93 | 11.09 | 14.19 | 28.5 | 18.18 |
| 1972 | 17.5 | 10.79 | 13.33 | 26.95 | 16.28 |
| 1973 | 17.23 | 9.85 | 12.63 | 26.16 | 15.21 |
| 1974 | 16.76 | 9.5 | 12.22 | 22.43 | 13.84 |
| 1975 | 16.04 | 8.6 | 13.8 | 20.8 | 18.88 |
| 1976 | 14.47 | 8.3 | 12.53 | 18.9 | 17.11 |
| 1977 | 14.16 | 8.02 | 11.44 | 18.11 | 16.03 |
| 1978 | 13.26 | 7.76 | 10.65 | 17.06 | 15.25 |
| 1979 | 12.9 | 7.48 | 10.01 | 15.67 | 13.03 |
| 1980 | 12.1 | 6.9 | 10.01 | 15.67 | 13.03 |
| 1981 | 11.16 | 6.94 | 9.71 | 13.99 | 12.48 |
| 1982 | 10.98 | 6.82 | 9.46 | 12.72 | 11.42 |
| 1983 | 10.2 | 7.03 | 9.13 | 12.07 | 10.89 |
| 1984 | 9.61 | 6.4 | 8.29 | 11.22 | 9.87 |
| 1985 | 9.36 | 6.74 | 8.31 | 10.34 | 8.92 |
| 1986 | 9.51 | 5.9 | 8.04 | 10.06 | 9.2 |
| 1987 | 9.12 | 6.12 | 7.84 | 9.6 | 8.88 |
| 1988 | 8.97 | 5.82 | 7.84 | 9.18 | 8.05 |
| 1989 | 8.42 | 5.77 | 7.54 | 8.59 | 7.78 |
| 1990 | 7.85 | 5.96 | 7.34 | 8.01 | 7.6 |
| 1991 | 7.35 | 6.09 | 7.26 | 8.22 | 7.19 |
| 1992 | 6.58 | 5.19 | 6.82 | 7.91 | 7.05 |
| 1993 | 6.34 | 4.79 | 6.47 | 7.09 | 6.69 |
| 1994 | 6.19 | | 5.9 | | |

*Source:* Taken from WHO Health for All database and compiled by Professor Martin McKee.

Table 4 *Number of people insured and payments for private health care – BUPA, PPP and WPA (United Kingdom)*

| | Subscribers 000s | Persons insured 000s | Subscriptions paid £m | Benefits paid £m | Persons insured Per subscriber | Per 1,000 UK population | As % UK population |
|---|---|---|---|---|---|---|---|
| 1955 | 274 | 585 | 2 | 2 | 2.1 | 11.5 | 1.1 |
| 1956 | 318 | 680 | 2 | 2 | 2.1 | 13.3 | 1.3 |
| 1957 | 354 | 755 | 3 | 2 | 2.1 | 14.7 | 1.5 |
| 1958 | 387 | 825 | 3 | 3 | 2.1 | 16.0 | 1.6 |
| 1959 | 419 | 895 | 4 | 3 | 2.1 | 17.2 | 1.7 |
| 1960 | 467 | 995 | 4 | 4 | 2.1 | 19.0 | 1.9 |
| 1961 | 504 | 1,070 | 5 | 4 | 2.1 | 20.3 | 2.0 |
| 1962 | 546 | 1,165 | 6 | 5 | 2.1 | 21.9 | 2.2 |
| 1963 | 587 | 1,250 | 7 | 6 | 2.1 | 23.3 | 2.3 |
| 1964 | 632 | 1,345 | 8 | 7 | 2.1 | 24.9 | 2.5 |
| 1965 | 680 | 1,445 | 9 | 8 | 2.1 | 26.6 | 2.7 |
| 1966 | 735 | 1,565 | 11 | 9 | 2.1 | 28.6 | 2.9 |
| 1967 | 784 | 1,670 | 13 | 11 | 2.1 | 30.4 | 3.0 |
| 1968 | 831 | 1,770 | 14 | 12 | 2.1 | 32.1 | 3.2 |
| 1969 | 886 | 1,887 | 17 | 15 | 2.1 | 34.0 | 3.4 |
| 1970 | 930 | 1,982 | 20 | 17 | 2.1 | 35.6 | 3.6 |
| 1971 | 986 | 2,102 | 24 | 20 | 2.1 | 37.6 | 3.8 |
| 1972 | 1,021 | 2,176 | 29 | 24 | 2.1 | 38.8 | 3.9 |

Table 4 (cont.)

| | Subscribers 000s | Persons insured 000s | Subscriptions paid £m | Benefits paid £m | Per subscriber | Persons insured per 1,000 UK population | As % UK population |
|---|---|---|---|---|---|---|---|
| 1973 | 1,064 | 2,265 | 36 | 29 | 2.1 | 40.3 | 4.0 |
| 1974 | 1,096 | 2,334 | 45 | 36 | 2.1 | 41.5 | 4.2 |
| 1975 | 1,087 | 2,315 | 55 | 46 | 2.1 | 41.2 | 4.1 |
| 1976 | 1,057 | 2,251 | 71 | 53 | 2.1 | 40.0 | 4.0 |
| 1977 | 1,057 | 2,254 | 91 | 65 | 2.1 | 40.1 | 4.0 |
| 1978 | 1,118 | 2,338 | 105 | 68 | 2.1 | 42.5 | 4.3 |
| 1979 | 1,292 | 2,765 | 122 | 84 | 2.1 | 49.2 | 4.9 |
| 1980 | 1,647 | 3,577 | 154 | 128 | 2.2 | 63.5 | 6.4 |
| 1981 | 1,863 | 4,063 | 205 | 195 | 2.2 | 72.1 | 7.2 |
| 1982 | 1,917 | 4,182 | 286 | 245 | 2.2 | 74.3 | 7.4 |
| 1983 | 1,954 | 4,254 | 355 | 291 | 2.2 | 75.5 | 7.5 |
| 1984 | 2,010 | 4,367 | 413 | 341 | 2.2 | 77.3 | 7.7 |

*Laing and Buisson survey estimates for all insurers*

| | | | | | | | |
|---|---|---|---|---|---|---|---|
| 1985 | 2,380 | 5,057 | 520 | 456 | 2.1 | 89.3 | 8.9 |
| 1986 | 2,428 | 4,951 | 609 | 513 | 2.0 | 87.2 | 8.7 |
| 1987 | 2,590 | 5,282 | 711 | 581 | 2.0 | 87.2 | 8.7 |

| 1988 | 2,809 | 5,921 | 807 | 678 | 2.1 | 103.8 | 10.4 |
| 1989 | 3,052 | 6,267 | 945 | 809 | 2.1 | 109.5 | 10.9 |
| 1990 | 3,257 | 6,664 | 1,089 | 977 | 2.0 | 116.1 | 11.6 |
| 1991 | 3,472 | 7,049 | 1,253 | 1,137 | 2.0 | 122.5 | 12.2 |

*Notes:*

BUPA = British United Provident Association

PPP = Private Patients Plan

WPA = Western Provident Association

*Sources:* Lee Donaldson Associates (1950–73) and Laing and Buisson.

Taken from Office of Health Economics (OHE), *Compendium of Health Statistics* (London: OHE, 8th edn, 1992).

Table 5 *Availability of hospital beds, 1959–1992 (thousands)*

| | Acute service | | | Mental illness | Mental handicap[b] | Geriatrics[c] | All beds[d] | Per 1,000 population | |
| | Medical | Surgical | Total[a] | | | | | Total acute | All beds |
| --- | --- | --- | --- | --- | --- | --- | --- | --- | --- |
| 1959 | 89 | 89 | 183 | 178 | 64 | 62 | 546 | 3.6 | 10.8 |
| 1960 | 85 | 92 | 182 | 175 | 66 | 63 | 543 | 3.6 | 10.6 |
| 1961 | 83 | 91 | 179 | 173 | 65 | 62 | 542 | 3.5 | 10.5 |
| 1962 | 82 | 92 | 179 | 170 | 66 | 63 | 537 | 3.5 | 10.4 |
| 1963 | 80 | 92 | 177 | 167 | 67 | 64 | 535 | 3.4 | 10.3 |
| 1964 | 79 | 93 | 177 | 166 | 69 | 64 | 536 | 3.4 | 10.2 |
| 1965 | 79 | 93 | 177 | 164 | 69 | 65 | 534 | 3.4 | 10.1 |
| 1966 | 78 | 93 | 176 | 162 | 68 | 65 | 531 | 3.3 | 10.0 |
| 1967 | 76 | 94 | 175 | 160 | 69 | 66 | 531 | 3.3 | 10.0 |
| 1968 | 75 | 94 | 174 | 157 | 69 | 67 | 528 | 3.3 | 9.9 |
| 1969 | 73 | 94 | 172 | 154 | 69 | 68 | 524 | 3.2 | 9.7 |
| 1970 | 70 | 98 | 171 | 151 | 69 | 69 | 519 | 3.2 | 9.6 |
| 1971 | 72 | 100 | 180 | 146 | 68 | 70 | 513 | 3.3 | 9.4 |
| 1972 | 71 | 99 | 176 | 141 | 67 | 70 | 506 | 3.2 | 9.3 |
| 1973 | 69 | 98 | 170 | 135 | 66 | 70 | 499 | 3.1 | 9.1 |
| 1974 | 68 | 98 | 169 | 130 | 65 | 69 | 489 | 3.1 | 8.9 |
| 1975 | 67 | 96 | 165 | 124 | 64 | 70 | 480 | 3.0 | 8.8 |
| 1976 | 66 | 97 | 168 | 121 | 63 | 70 | 472 | 3.1 | 8.6 |
| 1977 | 65 | 96 | 164 | 117 | 62 | 71 | 463 | 3.0 | 8.5 |
| 1978 | 63 | 97 | 163 | 112 | 60 | 72 | 454 | 3.0 | 8.3 |
| 1979 | 63 | 97 | 157 | 111 | 59 | 71 | 446 | 2.9 | 8.2 |

| | | | | | | | | | |
|---|---|---|---|---|---|---|---|---|---|
| 1980 | 62 | 96 | 158 | 110 | 58 | 71 | 441 | 2.9 | 8.0 |
| 1981 | 61 | 95 | 153 | 107 | 57 | 71 | 438 | 2.8 | 8.0 |
| 1982 | 60 | 94 | 151 | 106 | 56 | 72 | 436 | 2.8 | 8.0 |
| 1983 | 60 | 93 | 167 | 104 | 55 | 72 | 429 | 3.0 | 7.8 |
| 1984 | 59 | 91 | 162 | 100 | 53 | 72 | 414 | 3.0 | 7.5 |
| 1985 | 58 | 88 | 160 | 97 | 50 | 72 | 405 | 2.9 | 7.3 |
| 1986 | 58 | 86 | 157 | 93 | 47 | 71 | 394 | 2.9 | 7.1 |
| 1987/8 | 57 | 85 | 153 | 87 | 41 | 71 | 373 | 2.8 | 7.1 |
| 1988/9 | 55 | 82 | 147 | 82 | 37 | 67 | 357 | 2.7 | 6.7 |
| 1989/90 | 53 | 78 | 146 | 78 | 33 | 65 | 342 | 2.6 | 6.4 |
| 1990/1 | 49 | 73 | 142 | 73 | 29 | 61 | 325 | 2.5 | 6.1 |
| 1991/2 | 45 | 66 | 139 | 70 | 27 | 60 | 314 | 2.5 | 5.6 |

*Notes:* In compiling tables for Great Britain from statistics for England and Wales and for Scotland, figures have been added together which are not all on precisely the same basis in definition or timing (e.g. from calendar to financial year ending 31 March from 1987/8). However, the differences do not affect the broad picture of the health services shown for Great Britain by these figures. From 1988/9 onwards, both the acute medical and surgical beds in England have been estimated from total acute beds.

[a] Including pre-convalescent, gynaecology and other specialist beds.
[b] Including severe mental handicap.
[c] Including units for younger disabled.
[d] Figures include obstetrics and other departments not shown in the table.

*Sources:* Health and Personal Social Services Statistics for England, Wales and Scotland.
Taken from Office of Health Economics (OHE) *Compendium of Health Statistics* (London: OHE, 8th edn, 1992).

# References

Abraham, J. 1995. *Science, Politics and the Pharmaceutical Industry: Controversy and Bias in Drug regulation*. London: UCL Press. Useful study of a neglected, but important area of health policy.

Allsop, J. 1995a. *Health Policy and the NHS. Towards 2000*. London: Longman, 2nd edn. Survey which focuses on recent events.

    1995b. 'Health: from seamless service to patchwork quilt', in Gladstone, 1995, pp. 98–123. Chapter which dissects some of the key issues in health policy, with a more recent focus.

Anderson, S. and Berridge, V., forthcoming. 'The chemist's story: the role of the community pharmacist in health and welfare 1911 to 1986', in J. Bornat, R. Perks *et al.*, *Oral History in Health and Welfare*. London: Routledge.

Armstrong, D. 1983. *Political Anatomy of the Body: medical knowledge in Britain in the twentieth century*. Cambridge University Press. Analysis of key developments in twentieth-century health, general practice and the survey among them.

Baggott, R. 1990. *Alcohol, Politics and Social Policy*. Aldershot: Avebury. A neglected topic.

    1994. *Health and Health Care in Britain*. Basingstoke: Macmillan. Survey volume with emphasis on recent events.

Baldwin, S. and Twigg, J. 1991. 'Women and community care-reflections on a debate', in M. Maclean and D. Groves (eds.), *Women's Issues in Social Policy*. London: Routledge, pp. 117–35.

Baly, M. 1986. *A History of the Queen's Institute: 100 years, 1887–1987*. London: Croom Helm.

Barnett, C. 1986. *The Audit of War: The Illusion and Reality of Britain as a Great Nation*. London: Macmillan.

Bartley, M. 1994 'The relationship between research and policy:

the case of unemployment and health', in Oakley and Williams, 1994, pp. 201–21. Stimulating account of the 1980s' debate and the withdrawal from it of 'official' public health. Raises important issues about epidemiology and health research.

Beinart, J. 1987. *A History of the Nuffield Department of Anaesthetics, Oxford, 1937–1987.* Oxford University Press. The institutional development of medical technology.

Benner, P. 1989. 'The early years of the National Health Service – an insider's view', in A. Gorst, L. Johnman and W. Scott-Lucas (eds.), *Post War Britain, 1945–64, Themes and Perspectives.* London: Pinter, pp. 43–52.

Berridge, V. 1996. *AIDS in the U.K.: The Making of Policy, 1981–1994.* Oxford University Press. Study of recent history which stresses consensual reaction amid 'Thatcher revolution'.

1997. 'Doctors and the state: the changing role of medical expertise in policy making', *Contemporary British History*, 11 (4), pp. 66–85. The changed role of medical expertise in central government.

1998. 'Science and policy: the case of post-war smoking policy', in S. Lock, Reynolds and E. M. Tansey (eds.), *Ashes to Ashes.* Amsterdam: Rodopi, pp. 143–63.

1999. 'Passive smoking and its pre-history: policy speaks to science?', *Social Science and Medicine.*

Black, N. 1997. 'A national strategy for research and development: lessons from England', *Annual Review of Public Health*, 18, pp. 485–505.

Blaxter, M. 1990. *Health and Lifestyles.* London: Tavistock, Routledge. Investigation into health beliefs and behaviours.

1997. 'Whose fault is it? People's own conceptions of the reasons for health inequalities', *Social Science and Medicine*, 44 (6), pp. 747–56.

Blythe, M. 1986. 'A century of health education', *Health and Hygiene*, 7, pp. 105–15. One of the few published surveys of health education history.

Bourke, J. 1994. *Working Class Cultures in Britain, 1890–1960: Gender, Class and Ethnicity.* London: Routledge. Downplays comfortable notions of working-class 'community'.

Bridgen, P. and Lowe, R. 1998. *Welfare Policy under the Conservatives, 1951–64.* (London: PRO). Invaluable guide.

Brookes, B. 1988. *Abortion in England, 1900–1967.* Beckenham: Croom Helm.

Bryder, L. 1999. 'We shall not find salvation in inoculation: BCG vaccination in Scandinavia, Britain and the USA, 1921–1960', *Social Science and Medicine.*

Calnan, M. 1991. *Preventing Coronary Heart Disease: Prospects, Policies and Politics.* London: Routledge. Useful survey, semi-historical, of a key post-war health problem.

Campbell, J. 1987. *Nye Bevan and the Mirage of British Socialism.* London: Weidenfeld and Nicolson. Revisionist account of Bevan's achievement.

Charlton, J. and Murphy, M. (eds.) 1997. *The Health of Adult Britain, 1841–1994.* London: Stationery Office. Invaluable series of survey articles and data, covering a range of issues from diet to old age.

Charlton, J. and Quaife, K. 1997. 'Trends in diet, 1841–1994', in Charlton and Murphy, M. (eds.), pp. 93–113.

Cherry, S. 1996. *Medical services and the Hospitals in Britain, 1860–1939.* Cambridge University Press. Predecessor survey to this one, focusing usefully on hospitals and financing.

Cochrane, A. L. 1972. *Effectiveness and Efficiency: Random Reflections on Health Services.* London: Nuffield Provincial Hospitals Trust.

Cooter, R. 1995. 'The resistible rise of medical ethics', *Social History of Medicine,* 8, pp. 257–70. Controversial critique of the rise of ethics in the post-war years.

Cornwell, J. 1984. *Hard Earned Lives.* London: Tavistock. Anthropological account of working-class community.

Coulter, A. 1995. 'Evaluating general practice fundholding in the U.K.', *European Journal of Public Health,* 5(4), pp. 233–9.

Crossman, R. 1979. *The Crossman Diaries* (condensed version edited by A. Howard), London: Magnum.

Davenport-Hines, R. 1990. *Sex, Death and Punishment: Attitudes to Sex and Sexuality in Britain since the Renaissance.* London: Collins. Impassioned and wide-ranging account of changes in sexual and homosexual policy. One of the few research based accounts of these issues which encompasses the post-war period.

Davey, B. and Popay, J. (eds.) 1993. *Dilemmas in Health Care.* Buckingham: Open University Press. Valuable set of essays in user-friendly OU format, covering rationing, community care, technology, etc.

Dingwall, R., Rafferty, A.-M., and Webster, C. 1988. *An Introduction to the Social History of Nursing.* London: Routledge. Useful and wide-ranging survey, with main interest in nursing policy.

Dunnell, K. 1997. 'Are we healthier?', in Charlton and Murphy,

1997, pp. 173–81.

Eckstein, H. 1958. *The English Health Service: Its Origins, Structure and Achievements.* Cambridge, Mass.: Harvard University Press. Early account.

Edwards, B. 1995. *The National Health Service: A Manager's Tale, 1946–1994.* London: Nuffield Provincial Hospitals Trust. Edwards shows management in the NHS originated before the 1980s.

Esping-Anderson, G. 1990. *The Three Worlds of Welfare Capitalism.* Cambridge: Polity Press.

Finch, J. and Groves, D. 1983. *A Labour of Love: Women, Work and the Family.* London: Routledge.

Finlayson, G. 1994. *Citizen, State and Social Welfare in Britain, 1830–1990.* Oxford: Clarendon Press. Social policy focused account of voluntarism.

Florin, D. 1999. 'Scientific uncertainty and the role of expert advice: the case of health checks for coronary heart disease prevention by general practitioners', *Social Science and Medicine.*

Fox, D. 1986. *Health Policies, Health Politics: The British and American Experience, 1911–1965.* Princeton University Press. Study which stresses commonalities rather than divergences between health systems through the issue of regionalism.

Gladstone, D. (ed.) 1995. *British Social Welfare. Past, Present and Future.* London, UCL Press. Useful and wide-ranging set of recent survey essays.

Glennerster, H. 1995. *British Social Policy since 1945.* Oxford: Blackwell. Valuable survey volume which encompasses health.

Gould, T. 1995. *A Summer Plague: Polio and its Survivors.* New Haven and London: Yale University Press, 1995. History and personal account.

Graham, H. 1979. 'Prevention and health: every mothers' business. A comment on child health policies in the 1970s', in C. Harris (ed.), *The Sociology of the Family.* Keele, 1979, 160–85. Stresses foundation of prevention in women's work.

   1987. 'Womens' smoking and family health', *Social Science and Medicine*, 25, pp. 47–56. Key article which looks at smoking from the women's point of view.

Gray, A. 1993. 'International patterns of health care, 1960 to the 1990s', in Webster, 1993, pp. 172–92. Useful contextual piece.

Hall, P. 1986 'The development of Health Centres', in P. Hall, H. Land, R. Parker and A. Webb (eds.), *Change, Choice and*

*Conflict in Social Policy*. First published 1975; Aldershot: Gower; repr. pp. 277–310. Older article providing valuable survey of the health centre issue to the 1960s.

Ham, C. 1992. *Health Policy in Britain: The Politics and Organisation of the National Health Service*. Basingstoke: Macmillan, 3rd edn. Comprehensive review of service development, recently revised.

Harris, B. 1995. *The Health of the Schoolchild: A History of the School Medical Service in England and Wales*. Buckingham: Open University Press. Thorough history of a neglected service.

Harris, J. 1981. 'Some aspects of social policy in Britain during the Second World War', in W. Mommsen (ed.), *The Emergence of the Welfare State in Britain and Germany*. London: Croom Helm, pp. 247–52.

1983. 'Did British workers want the welfare state?', in J. Winter (ed.), *The Working Class in Modern British History: Essays in Honour of Henry Pelling*. Cambridge University Press, pp. 200–14. Shows the complexity of public attitudes.

Harrison, S. and Wistow, G. 1993. 'Managing health care: balancing interests and influence', in Davey and Popay, 1993, pp. 12–26.

Helman, C. 1990. *Culture, Health and Illness*. London: Wright, 2nd edn. Anthropologically focused survey of health beliefs and lay/ professional interactions.

Hills, J. (ed.) 1991. *The State of Welfare: The Welfare State in Britain since 1974*. Oxford: Clarendon Press. Stimulating and integrated study of post-war welfare with a health piece looking at inputs and outputs.

Holmes, R. 1993. 'Coronary heart disease: a cautionary tale', in Davey and Popay, 1993, pp. 165–83.

Honigsbaum, F. 1979. *The Division in British Medicine: A History of the Separation of General Practice from Hospital Care*. London: Kogan Page. Detailed account of the crucial divide.

Hunter, D. 1993. 'Care in the community: rhetoric or reality?', in Davey and Popay, 1993, pp. 121–42.

Jefferys, K. 1987. 'British politics and social policy during the Second World War', *Historical Journal*, 30, pp. 123–44. Stresses lack of consensus about health between Labour and the Conservatives during wartime.

Jefferys, M. (ed.) 1989. *Growing Old in the Twentieth Century*. London: Routledge. Useful series of historical essays on an important and controversial topic.

Jefferys, M. and Sachs, H. 1983. *Rethinking General Practice:*

*Dilemmas in Primary Medical Care.* London: Tavistock. Account of the 'new' general practice, based on extensive research on a group practice.

Jones, Harriet 1991. 'New tricks for an old dog? The Conservatives and social policy, 1951–55', in A. Gorst, L. Johnman and W. Scott-Lucas (eds.), *Contemporary British History, 1931–1961. Politics and the Limits of Policy.* London: Pinter. Downgrades post-war consensus.

1992. 'The Conservative party and the welfare state, 1942–55'. PhD. thesis, University of London. Shows clear differences between the parties on health and welfare.

Jones, Helen 1994. *Health and Society in Twentieth Century Britain.* London: Longman. Valuable survey volume which avoids service history and stresses health experiences, gender and ethnicity.

Jones, K. 1993. *Asylums and After: A Revised History of the Mental Health Services from the Early Eighteenth Century to the 1990s.* London: Athlone Press. Survey history which includes post-war period.

Karpf, A. 1988. *Doctoring the Media. The Reporting of Health and Medicine.* London: Routledge. Well-written and stimulating account of the media and health issues.

Kennedy, I. 1981. *The Unmasking of Medicine.* London: Allen and Unwin.

Klein, R. 1995. *The New Politics of the NHS.* London: Longman, 3rd edn. Updated analysis, stimulating and incisive from the political science point of view, but does not take account of newer historical work on consensus.

Larkin, G. 1993. 'The emergence of para-medical professions,' in W. Bynum and R. Porter (eds.), *Companion Encyclopaedia of the History of Medicine*, II. London: Routledge, pp. 1329–49.

Lawrence, G. (ed.) 1994. *Technologies of Modern Medicine.* London: Science Museum. Collection of essays on an important but historically underdeveloped area so far as health is concerned.

Le Fanu, J. 1994. *Preventionitis: The Exaggerated Claims of Health Promotion.* London: Social Affairs Unit. 'Radical right' attack on prevention.

Le Grand, J., Winter, D. and Woolley, F. 1991. 'The National Health Service: safe in whose hands?', in Hills, 1991, pp. 88–134.

Leathard, A. 1980. *The Fight for Family Planning: The Development of Family Planning Services in Britain, 1921–1974.* London: Macmillan.

Leichter, H. M. 1991. *Free to be Foolish: Politics and Health Promotion in the U.S. and Great Britain.* Princeton University Press.

Lewis, J. 1986. *What Price Community Medicine? The Philosophy, Practice and Politics of Public Health since 1919,* Brighton: Harvester/Wheatsheaf. Historical critique of the role of public health taking in its metamorphosis into community medicine.

1992a. 'Providers, "consumers" the state and the delivery of health care services in twentieth century Britain', in A. Wear (ed.), *Medicine in Society,* Cambridge University Press, pp. 317–45. Stimulating overview and analysis.

1992b. *Women in Britain since 1945: Women, Family, Work and the State in the Post War years.* Oxford: Blackwell. Useful survey.

1993. 'Developing the mixed economy of care: emerging issues for voluntary organisations', *Journal of Social Policy,* 2 (2), pp. 173–92.

1997. 'The changing meaning of the G.P. contract'. *British Medical Journal,* 314, pp. 895–8. Stresses the move from professional to entrepreneurial models of general practice.

Loudon, I. 1998. 'Maternal mortality, 1880–1950: Some regional and international comparisons.' *Social History of Medicine,* 1, pp. 185–228.

1991. 'On maternal and infant mortality, 1900–1960', *Social History of Medicine* 4, pp. 29–73.

Lowe, R. 1990. 'The Second World War, consensus and the foundation of the welfare state' *Twentieth Century British History,* 1, pp. 152–82. Supports post-war consensus – with modification.

Lowe, R. 1993. *The Welfare State in Britain since 1945.* Basingstoke: Macmillan. Valuable survey which includes health services and a guide to theories of policy formation.

Macintyre, S. 1997. 'The Black Report and beyond: what are the issues?', *Social Science and Medicine,* 44 (6), pp. 723–45. Exhaustively referenced and scholarly account of recent controversies and research.

MacNicol, J. 'The evacuation of schoolchildren', in H. L. Smith (ed.), *War and Social Change: British Society in the Second World War.* Manchester University Press, pp. 3–31. Revisionist paper which argues that evacuation did not lead to social solidarity.

McKeown, T. 1976. *The Modern Rise of Population.* London: Edward Arnold. Did medical advance really help?

MacNicol, J. and Blaikie, A. 1989. 'The politics of retirement,

1908–1948', in Jefferys 1989, pp. 21—42.

McPherson, K. and Coleman, D. 1988. 'Health', in A. H. Halsey (ed.), *British Social Trends since 1900. A Guide to the Changing Social Structure of Britain.* Basingstoke: Macmillan, 2nd edn, pp. 398–461. Valuable survey, although statistics now outdated.

Marks, L. 1999. 'Not just a statistic': the history of USA and UK policy over thrombotic disease and the oral contraceptive pill, 1960s-1970s', *Social Science and Medicine.*

Marks, L. and Worboys, M. 1997. *Migrants, Minorities and Health.* London: Routledge. Collection of essays on neglected topic of ethnic health – with some post-war material.

Marsh, A. and McKay, S. 1994. *Poor Smokers.* London: Policy Studies Institute. Study which pointed to poverty implications of 'healthy' smoking policies.

Martin, M. 1995. 'Medical knowledge and medical practice: geriatric medicine in the 1950s', *Social History of Medicine*, 8 (3), pp. 443–61. Development of a new medical speciality.

Micale, M. and Porter, R. (eds.) 1994. *Discovering the History of Psychiatry.* Oxford University Press. Some post-war comments.

Mohan, J. 1995. *A National Health Service? The Restructuring of Health Care in Britain since 1979.* London: Macmillan. Survey of recent developments, which argues that a national service is a thing of the past.

Murcott, A. 1994. 'Food and nutrition in post-war Britain', in Obelkevich and Catterall, pp. 155–64. Useful initial survey.

Oakley, A. and Ashton, J. (eds.) 1997, *The Gift Relationship.* London: LSE Press. Reissue of original study of blood donation, with additional post-war material on AIDS and milk banking.

Oakley, A. and Williams, S. (eds.) 1994. *The Politics of the Welfare State.* London: UCL Press. Valuable collection of essays which include several on health issues.

Obelkevich, J. and Catterall, P. (eds.) 1994. *Understanding Post War British Society.* London: Routledge. Historians tackle 'social history' relating to health rather than 'social policy' as usual.

Oddy, D. J. 1982. 'The health of the people', in T. Barker and M. Drake (eds.), *Population and Society in Britain, 1850–1980.* London: Batsford, pp. 121–39.

Parker, R. 1986. 'The struggle for clean air', in P. Hall, H. Land, R. Barker and A. Webb (eds.), *Change, Choice and Conflict in Social Policy.* First published 1975; Aldershot; Gower repr., pp. 371–407.

Pater, J. 1981. *The Making of the NHS*. London: King Edwards Hospital Fund for London. Survey by an insider.

Perkin, H. 1989. *The Rise of Professional Society: England since 1880*. London: Routledge.

Popay, J. and Williams, G. 1994. 'Local voices in the National Health Service: needs, effectiveness and sufficiency', in Oakley and Williams, 1994, pp. 75–97.

Porter, D. (ed.) 1997. *Social Medicine and Medical Sociology in the Twentieth Century*. Amsterdam: Rodopi.

Powell, M. 1997. 'An expanding service: municipal acute medicine in the 1930s', *Twentieth Century British History*, 8 (3), pp. 334–57.

Prochaska, F. 1988. *The Voluntary Impulse: Philanthropy in Modern Britain*. London: Faber and Faber. Stresses the importance of voluntarism – not just for health matters.

Riley, D. 1981. 'The Free Mothers: pronatalism and working women in industry at the end of the last war in Britain', *History Workshop Journal*, 11, pp. 59–118.

Rivett, G. 1998. *From Cradle to Grave: Fifty years of the NHS*. London: King's Fund.

Roberts, E. 1995. *Women and Families: An Oral History, 1940–1970*. Oxford: Blackwell. Valuable study of changing relationships in this period, based on oral sources.

Roberts, F. 1952. *The Cost of Health*. London: Turnstile Press.

Rose, G. 1992. *The Strategy of Preventive Medicine*. Oxford University Press. Epidemiologist stresses the whole population approach and its paradoxes for the individual.

Royle, E. 1994. 'Trends in post-war British social history ', in Obelkevich and Catterall, 1994, pp. 9–18.

Scull, A. 1989. *Social Order/Mental Disorder: Anglo-American Psychiatry in Historical Perspective*. London: Routledge.

Seale, C. 1994. 'Health and healing in an age of science', in C. Seale and S. Pattison (eds.), *Medical Knowledge: Doubt and Certainty*. Buckingham: Open University Press, pp. 7–27.

Smith, R. 1994. 'Elements of demographic change in Britain since 1945', in Obelkevich and Catterall, 1994, pp. 19–30.

Stacey, M. 1976. 'The health service consumer: a sociological misconception', *Sociological Review Monograph*, 22, The Sociology of the National Health Service. University of Keele, pp. 194–200. Early discussion of 'consumerism'.

1988. *The Sociology of Health and Healing.* London: Unwin Hyman. Historical survey written by a sociologist, with useful material on professional interrelationships.

Stanton, J. 1999. 'The cost of living: kidney dialysis, rationing and health economics in Britain, 1965–1996', *Social Science and Medicine.*

Stevens, R. 1966. *Medical Practice in Modern England: The Impact of Specialization and State Medicine.* New Haven and London: Yale University Press. British American comparison, which examines the differential development of health systems.

Strong, P. and Robinson, J. 1990. *The NHS – Under New Management.* Buckingham: Open University Press. Ethnographic study of the introduction of a new style of management in the 1980s.

Summerfield, P. 1984. *Women Workers in the Second World War.* London: Croom Helm.

Thane, P. 1989. 'History and the sociology of ageing', *Social History of Medicine*, 2, pp. 93–6. Critique of some misconceptions in discussions of ageing, including the concept of 'structured dependency'.

1990. 'The debate on the declining birth rate in Britain: the "menace" of an ageing population, 1920s–1950s', *Continuity and Change*, 5 (2), pp. 283–305. Shows how a 'problem' of ageing was constructed and stresses the positive aspects of an ageing population.

1993. 'Geriatrics', in W. Bynum and R. Porter (eds.) *Companion Encyclopaedia of the History of Medicine*, II, London: Routledge, pp. 1092–115.

Thom, B. and Berridge, V. 1995. 'Special units for common problems': the birth of alcohol treatment units in England', *Social History of Medicine*, 8 (1), pp. 75–93.

Thomson, D. 1986. 'Welfare and the historians', in L. Bonfield, R. M. Smith and K. Wrightson (eds.), *The World We Have Gained: Histories of Population and Social Structure.* Oxford: Basil Blackwell, pp. 355–78.

Timmins, N. 1995. *The Five Giants. A Biography of the Welfare State.* London: Harper Collins. Gripping and wide-ranging account, using interviews with politicians and others.

Tinker, A. 1994. 'Old age and gerontology', in Obelkevich and Catterall, 1994, pp. 73–84.

Titmuss, R. 1950. *Problems of Social Policy.* London: HMSO. Classic study which stresses the impact of war.

Townsend, P. 1962. *The Last Refuge.* London: Routledge.

Townsend, P. and Davidson, N., Whitehead, M. 1988. *Inequalities in Health: The Black Report and the Health Divide.* London: Penguin.

Tranter, N. 1996. *British Population in the Twentieth Century.* London: Macmillan.

Tudor Hart, J. 1988. *A New Kind of Doctor: The General Practitioner's Part in the Health of the Community.* London: Merlin. History of the development of post-war general practice written by a key participant.

Unsworth, C. 1987. *The Politics of Mental Health Legislation.* Oxford: Clarendon Press. Useful study of the issue up to the 1980s.

Watkin, B. 1978. *The National Health Service: The First Phase, 1948–74 and After.* London: George Allen and Unwin.

Weatherall, M. 1993. 'Drug therapies', in W. Bynum and R. Porter (eds.), *Companion Encyclopaedia of the History of Medicine,* II. London: Routledge, pp. 915–38.

Webster, C. 1988a. *The Health Services since the War,* I. *Problems of Health Care. The National Health Service before 1957.* London: HMSO.

1988b. 'Labour and the origins of the National Health Service', in N. Rupke (ed.), *Science, Politics and the Public Good: Essays in Honour of Margaret Gowing.* London: Macmillan, pp. 184–202.

1990. 'Conflict and consensus: explaining the British health service', *Twentieth Century British History,* 1, pp. 115–51. Stresses the importance of civil servants and the labour movement.

1991. 'The elderly and the early National Health Service', in M. Pelling and R. Smith (eds.), *Life, Death and the Elderly: Historical Perspectives.* London: Routledge, pp. 165–93.

1994. 'Conservatives and consensus: the politics of the National Health Service, 1951–64', in Oakley and Williams, 1994, pp. 54–74. Scepticism about post-war consensus.

1996. *The Health Services since the War,* II. *Government and Health Care – The British National Health Service, 1958–1979.* London: The Stationery Office. The official history, an extensive analysis of previously unused primary sources.

1998. *The NHS: A Political History.* Oxford University Press.

Webster, C. (ed.) 1993. *Caring for Health: History and Diversity.* Milton Keynes: Open University Press. Survey with broad chronological and geographical range.

Weeks, J. 1981. *Sex, Politics and Society: The Regulation of Sexuality since 1800.* London: Longman. Valuable survey which encompasses post-war developments from the perspective of a historian-participant.

Welshman, J. 1996. 'In search of the "problem family": public health and social work in England and Wales, 1940–1970', *Social History of Medicine*, 9, pp. 447–65. Contribution to discussion of decline of public health.

Welshman, J. 1998 'Evacuation and social policy during the Second World War: myth and reality', *Twentieth Century British History*, 9(1), pp. 28–53. Revises MacNicol's pessimism about the effect of evacuation.

Williams, R. E. O. 1985. *Microbiology for the Public Health*. London: Public Health Laboratory Service. Participant account of an important but neglected area of health services.

Winter, J. 1983. 'Unemployment, nutrition and infant mortality in Britain, 1920–1950', in J. Winter (ed.), *The Working Class in Modern British History: Essays in Honour of Henry Pelling*. Cambridge University Press, pp. 100–20.

Young, M. and Willmott, P. 1957. *Family and Kinship in East London*. London: Routledge and Kegan Paul. Classic study which stresses the disruptive effect of rehousing on 'traditional' community ties.

# Index

# New Studies in Economic and Social History

*Titles in the series available from Cambridge University Press*

line', 1870–1970

*Previously published as*

**Studies in Economic and Social History**

*Titles in the series available from the Macmillan Press Limited*

---

# Economic History Society

The Economic History Society, which numbers around 3,000 members, publishes the *Economic History Review* four times a year (free to members) and holds an annual conference.

Enquiries about membership should be addressed to

The Assistant Secretary
Economic History Society
PO Box 70
Kingswood
Bristol
BS15 5TB

Full-time students may join at special rates.